SHAPE

-------- by --------

SHAPE

Free-Motion Quilting with Angela Walters

70+ Designs for Blocks, Backgrounds & Borders

stashBOOKS®

an imprint of C&T Publishing

Text copyright © 2014 by Angela Walters

Photography and Artwork copyright © 2014 by C&T Publishing, Inc.

Publisher: Amy Marson

Creative Director: Gailen Runge

Art Director: Kristy Zacharias

Editor: Liz Aneloski

Technical Editor: Sadhana Wray

Cover/Book Designer: April Mostek

Production Coordinator: Jenny Davis

Production Editor: Joanna Burgarino

Illustrator: Wendy Mathson

Photo Assistant: Mary Peyton Peppo

Styled photography by Nissa Brehmer and instructional photography by Diane Pedersen, unless otherwise noted

Published by Stash Books, an imprint of C&T Publishing, Inc., P.O. Box 1456, Lafayette, CA 94549

Library of Congress Cataloging-in-Publication Data

Walters, Angela, 1979-

 Shape by shape free-motion quilting with Angela Walters : 70+ designs for blocks, backgrounds & borders / Angela Walters.

    pages cm

 Includes index.

 ISBN 978-1-60705-788-8 (soft cover)

 1. Quilting--Patterns. 2. Patchwork--Patterns. 3. Patchwork quilts. 4. Shapes. I. Title.

 TT835.W35656 2014

 746.46--dc23

                          2014004191

Printed in China

10 9 8 7 6 5 4 3 2 1

CONTENTS

DEDICATION

To my husband, Jeremy. Who knew that the first quilt I made for you would turn into all of this?

ACKNOWLEDGMENTS

Sometimes I am overwhelmed by the number of great people I am blessed to be surrounded by. They have helped me every step of the way, and I couldn't have done this without them!

To Jessica and Ruth, my friends and partners in this crazy endeavor. You keep me on track and sane. I'm so blessed to have you in my life.

To Kathy Limpic and Kristi Ryan, who pieced the beautiful quilts. Thanks for contributing your skills to this book.

And finally, a huge thanks to all the people at C&T, who have been so great to work with. This book wouldn't be what it is without you.

INDEX
OF QUILTING DESIGNS

SQUARES

Square 1
(page 14)

Square 2
(page 16)

Square 3
(page 18)

Square 4
(page 20)

Square 5
page 21)

Square 6
(page 22)

Square 7
(page 23)

Square 8
(page 24)

Square 9
(page 25)

Square 10
(page 26)

TRIANGLES

Triangle 1
(page 30)

Triangle 2
(page 31)

Triangle 3
(page 32)

Triangle 4
(page 33)

Triangle 5
(page 34)

Triangle 6
(page 35)

Triangle 7
(page 36)

Triangle 8
(page 37)

Triangle 9
(page 38)

Triangle 10
(page 39)

CIRCLES

Circle 1
(page 42)

Circle 2
(page 43)

Circle 3
(page 44)

Circle 4
(page 45)

Circle 5
(page 46)

Circle 6
(page 47)

Circle 7
(page 48)

Circle 8
(page 49)

Circle 9
(page 50)

Circle 10
(page 51)

DIAMONDS

Diamond 1
(page 54)

Diamond 2
(page 55)

Diamond 3
(page 56)

Diamond 4
(page 57)

Diamond 5
(page 58)

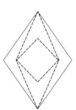

Diamond 6
(page 60)

Diamond 7
(page 62)

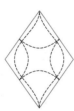

Diamond 8
(page 63)

Diamond 9
(page 64)

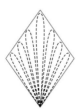

Diamond 10
(page 65)

HEXAGONS

Hexagon 1
(page 68)

Hexagon 2
(page 70)

Hexagon 3
(page 72)

Hexagon 4
(page 74)

Hexagon 5
(page 75)

Hexagon 6
(page 76)

Hexagon 7
(page 78)

Hexagon 8
(page 79)

Hexagon 9
(page 80)

Hexagon 10
(page 81)

NEGATIVE SPACE

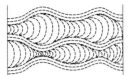

Signature Design
(page 84)

Peapods
(page 86)

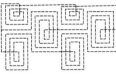

Offset Squares
(page 88)

Swirl Chain
(page 90)

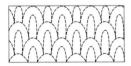

Links
(page 92)

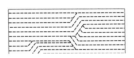

Merged Lines
(page 94)

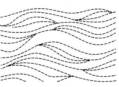

Wavy Wavy
(page 96)

Jumbled Lines
(page 98)

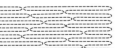

Back-and-Forth Lines
(page 100)

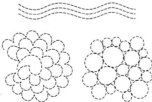

Improv Quilting
(page 102)

BORDERS

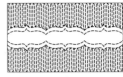

Herringbone
(page 106)

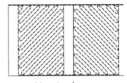

Brackets
(page 108)

Triangles
(page 110)

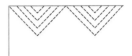

Half Brackets
(page 112)

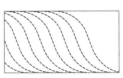

Serpentine Line
(page 114)

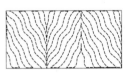

Wavy Variation
(page 116)

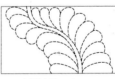

Wild Feathers
(page 118)

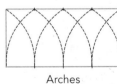

Arches
(page 120)

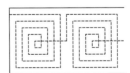

Square Chain
(page 122)

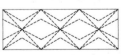

Dot-to-Dot Borders
(page 124)

INTRODUCTION

Do you ever suffer from quilter's amnesia? It's what happens when you think you're ready to machine quilt your quilt top, but you seem to have forgotten all of your favorite quilting designs! Is anything more frustrating? I have been machine quilting for more than ten years, and I still get quilter's amnesia. This book has given me the perfect opportunity to pull together my favorite quilting designs. The designs range from classic free-motion quilting designs to modern interpretations of other quilting designs.

My objective for this book is twofold. Of course, I hope you will find new quilting designs that will appeal to you. But my main hope is that you will keep this book handy in your quilting area. When the dreaded quilter's amnesia strikes, you can flip through and find ideas and inspiration in these pages.

What's Inside

To make this book as user-friendly as possible, it is divided into three sections, each addressing a different part of a quilt: Blocks, Negative Space, and Borders. Breaking down a quilt into basic components can help you decide what quilting designs to use, and where. Each section in the book contains quilting designs with photos and step-by-step illustrations as well as design variations, tips, and pointers for applying these ideas in your quilt design.

Adapt the Designs to Other Shapes

The quilting designs are shown using a specific geometric shape, but there's no reason to limit yourself to that shape. Try adapting the design to fit other shapes. If you can't find the right design in one chapter, look to other chapters for inspiration. Using these designs in several different ways, making them work double-duty, will mean you are getting the most out of this book! The possibilities are endless.

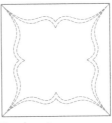

Brackets in a square
(page 22)

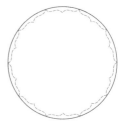

Brackets in a circle
(page 51)

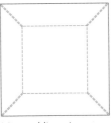

Mitered lines in a square (page 16)

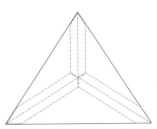

Mitered lines in a triangle
(page 33)

Ready to quilt? Let's go!

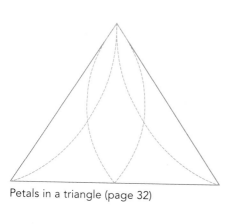

Petals in a triangle (page 32)

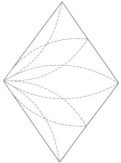

Petals in a diamond
(page 54)

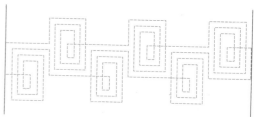

Offset squares in negative space (page 88)

Offset squares in a border (page 122)

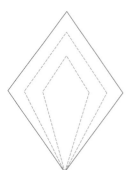

Echo lines in a
diamond (page 55)

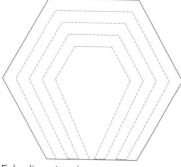

Echo lines in a hexagon (page 74)

Each pair of illustrations shows how
the same design looks when used
in different shapes. Notice how the
enclosing shape changes the look of
the design in subtle or dramatic ways.

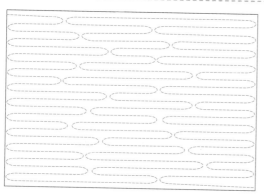

Back-and-forth in negative space (page 100)

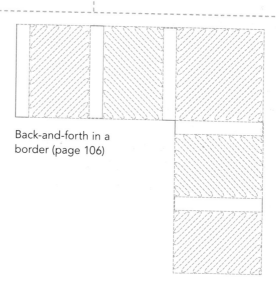

Back-and-forth in a
border (page 106)

section 1:
QUILT BLOCKS

SQUARES 12

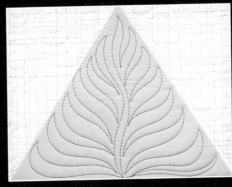

TRIANGLES 28

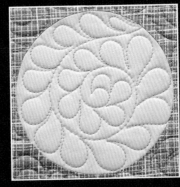

CIRCLES 40

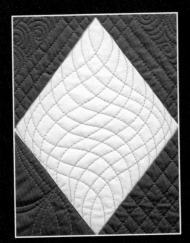

DIAMONDS 52

HEXAGONS 66

Ahhh...quilt blocks.

They can account for most of the area to be quilted, and yet I get tripped up when deciding what quilting designs to use for blocks. In this section, I share some of my favorite designs to use in quilt blocks in commonly found shapes: squares, triangles, circles, diamonds, and hexagons. I have tried to present designs to fill a range of needs. Almost every design includes a variation, and my hope is that you will find a design that works for your quilt.

As you flip through the following chapters, you'll see that block size can help guide your design choices. For example, some quilting designs might not provide enough coverage to fill a large block, and other designs might be too tight for a small block. What do I mean by small, medium, and large? It varies, but in general small is about 2″–4″, medium is about 5″–8″, and I'd say large is anything bigger. Keep in mind these are ballparks and can change as your skill grows. Also, the variations can help you adjust the design for your block size.

While I can't possibly imagine all the shapes that make up every quilt block, I hope this section will serve as inspiration. Ready? Let's get started!

note The ideas and information presented in this book can stand alone, but if you'd like more background on machine quilting basics, especially for use with modern quilts, see my first book *Free-Motion Quilting with Angela Walters: Choose & Use Quilting Designs on Modern Quilts,* also from Stash Books.

SQUARES
(AND RECTANGLES)

Pieced by Kathy Limpic and quilted by Angela Walters

It would seem that choosing a design for a square block would be simple. It is, after all, the most basic shape. But more than once, I have stared at a quilt top and not known what to do with the squares. Do I want something with a more complex look? Something clean and simple? Regardless of the look you are going for, this chapter will help get you on the right track.

Squares and rectangles are similar in shape, and I have opted to demonstrate the designs in square shapes. However, any of them can easily be modified for rectangles.

Tips for Quilting Squares

BREAK UP LARGER SQUARE BLOCKS INTO SMALLER SQUARES.

You will find that quite a few of the designs in this chapter divide blocks into smaller shapes. This makes it easier to manage larger squares or rectangles, especially if you are quilting on a home sewing machine. It can also add complexity to plain squares, resulting in quilting that is fun to look at.

CHECK OUT OTHER CHAPTERS IN THIS SECTION.

Most of the designs in this section can be adapted for squares and rectangles, especially the designs shown for circles. If you can't find the right design in this chapter, look to other chapters for inspiration. Making the designs work double-duty will mean that you are getting the most out of this book.

LOOK AT THE WHOLE QUILT.

Sometimes it's easier to look at each block as a separate entity. But if you're stumped on which designs to use on your quilt, look at the blocks as part of a bigger picture. Is there a way you can use the quilting designs to pull the blocks all together? Can you quilt designs to form secondary patterns, such as grids, on your quilt? Asking yourself these questions will help you decide on the best designs for your quilt.

Can you use different designs within the same block? For example, if you're quilting Rail Fence blocks, consider quilting each strip in a different design, giving a simple block a more complex look.

USE THE DESIGNS IN THE CHAPTER IN DIFFERENT WAYS.

There is no reason to limit these designs to squares and rectangular blocks. Try adapting them to fit other shapes, including circles. You can also use these designs in borders—just divide the border into squares and repeat the designs. The same goes for quilt backgrounds (negative space). Using these designs in several different ways will mean that you are getting the most out of this chapter!

SQUARE 1

THIS DESIGN WILL GIVE YOUR SQUARE QUILT BLOCKS A GROOVY LOOK USING ONLY STRAIGHT LINES. IT STARTS FROM OUTSIDE THE BLOCK AND ENDS IN THE CENTER, WHICH MEANS YOU'LL NEED TO START EACH BLOCK SEPARATELY. WHILE THAT IS NORMALLY AGAINST MY GET-IT-DONE-QUICKLY QUILTING PHILOSOPHY, THIS DESIGN IS WORTH THE EXTRA EFFORT.

TIP

This design is also handy for quilting rectangles.

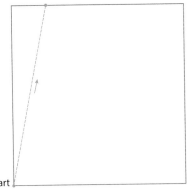

Start

1. Starting from a corner, quilt a straight line ending about 1″ from the next corner.

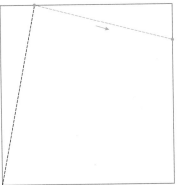

2. Quilt another straight line ending about 1″ from the next corner.

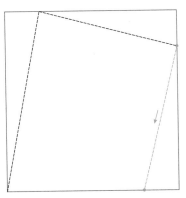

3. Repeat Step 2 to add a third line.

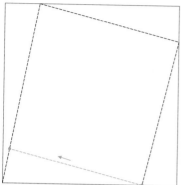

4. Quilt the fourth line just as you did the others, ending on the first line you quilted about 1″ from the corner.

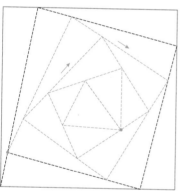

5. Repeat Steps 1–4, quilting your way into the center of the square.

VARIATIONS

For larger squares or for denser quilting, you can quilt the lines closer together. Simply move the endpoint closer to the corner, say ¼″ or ½″ from the corner instead of 1″.

Moving the lines closer together will help fill in larger quilt blocks better.

If straight lines aren't your cup of tea, try wavy lines instead.

Trade straight lines for wavy lines for a fun variation.

SQUARE 2

SOME QUILTS JUST BEG FOR A GEOMETRIC, MINIMALIST QUILTING DESIGN. THE MITERED CORNERS OF THIS DESIGN ALLOW YOU TO GET INTO THE BLOCK AND BACK OUT WITHOUT ANY OF THOSE PESKY STARTS AND STOPS. THIS DESIGN IS BEST FOR SMALLER SQUARES OR BLOCKS WHERE YOU WANT MINIMAL QUILTING.

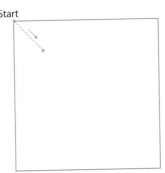

1. Starting at the outer corner, quilt a line diagonally toward the center, stopping about 1″ from the corner.

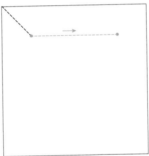

2. From that point, quilt a line parallel to the side of the block, stopping 1″ from the outside of the square.

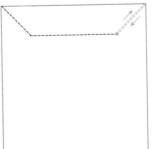

3. Quilt a line diagonally up to the corner of the block and back down the diagonal.

TIP

Don't let the fact that the design has traveling stop you from trying it. Using a thread color that blends with the fabric will help hide any imperfections.

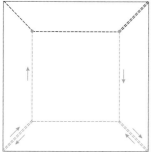

4. Repeat Steps 2 and 3 to quilt the next 2 sides of the block, stopping at the last corner of the inner square.

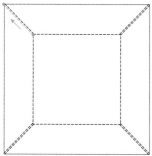

5. At this point, quilt along the first diagonal line, returning to the original starting point.

VARIATIONS

If this design leaves you wishing for a little more, try adding to it. Before quilting the last diagonal line, fill the inner square with a different design of your choice.

Try a simple continuous-curve design, or a classic free-motion quilting design such as swirls.

Adding curved lines from corner to corner inside the center square is an easy way to add to this design.

Use a free-motion quilting design, such as swirls, to create a variation of this design.

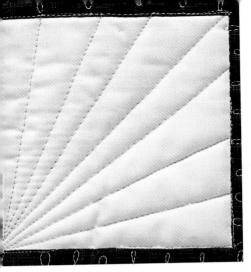

SQUARE 3

WHO KNEW THAT STRAIGHT LINES COULD "SOFTEN" A BLOCK? THE FAN DESIGN IS IDEAL FOR SMALL TO MEDIUM SQUARES. I USE IT ON SQUARE BLOCKS WHEN I WANT TO SOFTEN THE EDGES, ESPECIALLY IF THE BLOCK WILL BE PLACED ON A CORNER. TRY USING THIS DESIGN IN DIFFERENT AREAS, SUCH A BORDER CORNER OR IN A FOUR-PATCH QUILT BLOCK.

THIS TYPE OF DESIGN APPEARS TO BE SELF-EXPLANATORY, BUT I HANDLE THE QUILTING A LITTLE DIFFERENTLY, TRAVELING ALONG THE EDGES OF THE BLOCK RATHER THAN BACK-TRACKING IN THE LINES OF THE FAN.

1. Start from the corner where you want the bottom of the fan to be. Quilt a line to the opposite corner.

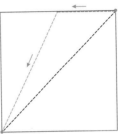

2. Travel along the top of the block until you are approximately at the midpoint, and quilt a line back to the starting point.

note Dividing the sides of the block into halves will allow you to quilt the design somewhat evenly without having to mark everything.

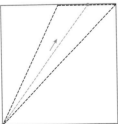

3. Quilt another diagonal line spaced halfway between the lines you quilted in Steps 1 and 2.

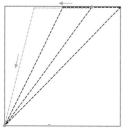

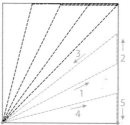

4. Travel across the top of the block until you get about a quarter of the way from the corner. Quilt a line down to the starting point.

5. Quilt the other side of the square as shown.

VARIATIONS

For larger squares, try combining the fan with a different design. For instance, in the picture below, I divided a large square into four sections. I quilted two of the smaller squares with the fan design and the other two with curved lines.

Need a little movement in your quilting? Try alternating straight lines with wavy lines to give this design a dynamic look.

Don't limit yourself to squares—you can easily adapt this design for other shapes. For instance, try quilting the fan design in triangular blocks.

Divide large squares and use the fan design in opposite corners.

Try quilting this design with straight and wavy lines.

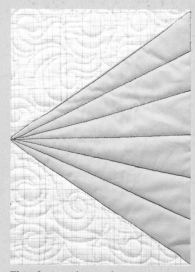

This design also works in triangular blocks.

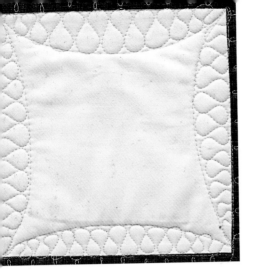

WHEN QUILTING A DESIGN IN ANY SHAPE BLOCK, I AM ALWAYS THINKING OF HOW I MIGHT ADD TO IT, WHETHER IT'S BY COMBINING DESIGNS OR FILLING IN UNUSED SPACE. THIS DESIGN IS A PERFECT EXAMPLE OF THAT. IT STARTS WITH THE BASIC CONTINUOUS-CURVE DESIGN AND ADDS THE RIBBON CANDY DESIGN. THE RESULT IS AN EXCELLENT DESIGN FOR MEDIUM-SIZED BLOCKS.

SQUARE 4

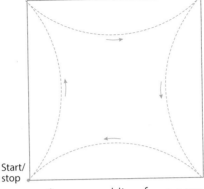

Start/stop

1. Starting at one corner, quilt a curved line from corner to corner until you arrive back at the starting point.

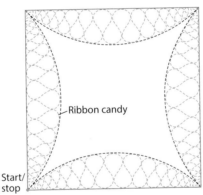

Ribbon candy

Start/stop

2. Fill in the space between the edge of the block and the curved line by quilting a ribbon candy design. Work your way around the block until you reach the starting point.

TIP

Even though I am using the ribbon candy design, you can consider other quilting designs. Experiment and find your favorite!

VARIATIONS

Depending on how large the square is, you can echo inside the first continuous-curve line a few times before adding the rest of the design.

SQUARE 5

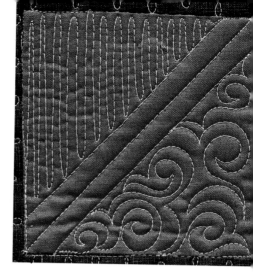

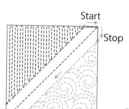

1. Quilt a straight line from one corner of a block to the opposite corner. Travel along the edge of the block approximately ¼″ and echo the line you just quilted until you end on the other side of the block about ¼″ from the starting point.

2. Quilt a dense back-and-forth line, filling in the top portion of the block.

3. Travel around the corner of the block until you are about ¼″ below the first line you quilted. Quilt a straight line to the opposite side of the block and fill in the area with a free-motion quilting design, such as swirls.

LIKE MOST OF THE QUILTING DESIGNS IN THIS BOOK, THIS DESIGN IS BASIC AND STRAIGHTFORWARD. HOWEVER, WHEN MULTIPLE SQUARES WITH THIS DESIGN ARE ARRANGED, THE DIAGONALS CREATE A SECONDARY PATTERN THAT CAN ADD HUGE INTEREST TO YOUR QUILT! IT FIRST DIVIDES THE SQUARE IN HALF DIAGONALLY AND THEN USES DIFFERENT QUILTING DESIGNS IN EACH HALF. I LOVE TO USE THIS DESIGN IN LARGER SQUARES, ALTERNATING THE DIRECTION OF THE LINES. IT CREATES A GRID-LIKE LOOK TO THE QUILTING THAT I JUST LOVE!

note When considering what designs to use in each section of the block, I try to pick designs that vary in style, line, or scale. This helps give the quilting contrast, which is something that I am particular about.

VARIATIONS

Experiment with this design by using different fillers in each side of the square. Pebbles and leaves are two great options.

Try using different quilting designs such as pebbles and leaves.

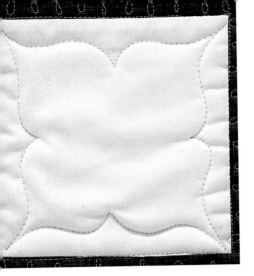

SQUARE 6

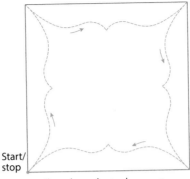

Start/
stop

THE BRACKET-SHAPED QUILTING DESIGN PROVIDES A QUICK AND EASY WAY TO WORK YOUR WAY AROUND A SQUARE, GIVING THE BLOCK A SLIGHTLY DIFFERENT LOOK FROM THE BASIC CONTINUOUS CURVE. I LIKE TO USE THIS DESIGN IN SMALLER BLOCKS. USING IT IN LARGER BLOCKS TENDS TO LEAVE TOO MUCH SPACE UNQUILTED IN THE CENTER, BUT THAT'S JUST MY PERSONAL PREFERENCE!

1. Starting from one corner, quilt a bracket shape to each corner, working your way around the quilt block.

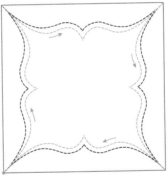

2. If you want to add more quilting in your quilt blocks, you can echo the brackets.

TIP

When I am quilting this design, I try to keep the "point" of the bracket halfway between the two corners. This helps me keep the design as symmetrical as possible.

VARIATIONS

An easy way to vary this design is to increase the distance between the echoed brackets, to fill in more of the square.

SQUARE 7

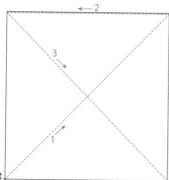

1. Starting from one corner, quilt a straight line diagonally to the opposite corner. Travel along the edge of the block until you reach the other corner. Quilt a line diagonally to the opposite corner.

note Not only do the crossed quilting lines add to the design, but they easily mark the center of the block for the next step.

THIS QUILTING DESIGN CREATES AN INTERESTING GRID WHEN USED IN ADJACENT SQUARES. IT COMBINES BOTH STRAIGHT AND CURVED LINES AND IS SO FAST AND EASY TO QUILT. ANOTHER BENEFIT OF THIS DESIGN IS THAT IT WORKS WELL IN SQUARES OF ALL SIZES.

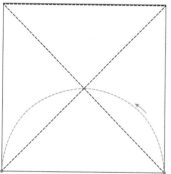

2. Quilt a curved line from the corner to the center of the block. Continue the curve to the next corner.

VARIATIONS

For larger blocks, you can echo the curves to fill in the block even more.

This design can be easily enhanced by echoing the curves.

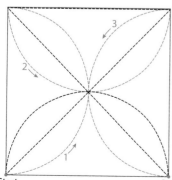

3. Continue working your way around the block until you return to the starting point.

SQUARE 8

WHEN CHOOSING QUILTING DESIGNS, I OFTEN USE ELEMENTS OF THE BLOCK ITSELF AS A PART OF THE DESIGN. THIS PARTICULAR DESIGN ECHOES TWO SIDES OF THE SQUARE AND IS WELL SUITED FOR MEDIUM TO LARGER BLOCKS. I LIKE TO USE THIS DESIGN FOR THE CORNER BLOCKS OF A LARGER DESIGN. THE BEST PART OF THIS DESIGN? IT IS COMPLETELY CUSTOMIZABLE, SO YOU CAN ADD AS MANY LINES AS YOU THINK IT NEEDS, AND EVEN CHANGE UP THE SPACING.

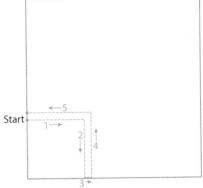

1. Start a few inches above a corner of the block. Quilt a horizontal line for that same distance and then quilt down to the bottom of the block. Travel along the side about ¼″ and echo the lines.

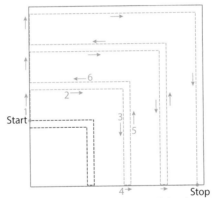

2. Repeat the first step, traveling along the side of the block and quilting straight lines.

VARIATIONS

For greater intensity, fill in between the lines with a different quilting design such as back-and-forth lines or pebbles.

Quilt pebbles between the straight lines for a variation of this design.

SQUARE 9

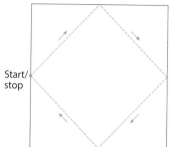

Start/stop

1. Starting from the midpoint of one side of the block, quilt a square on point. Try to place the points of the square at the midpoint of each side, ending at the starting point.

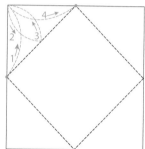

2. Fill in the first triangle section. Quilt a line curving to the corner of the block, out to the middle of the side of the on-point square, back to the corner, then to the midpoint of the next side.

WHEN WORKING WITH LARGER SQUARES, I OFTEN START BY DIVIDING THE AREA TO BE QUILTED INTO SMALLER SHAPES. NOT ONLY DOES THIS MAKE THE QUILTING MORE INTERESTING, BUT IT ALSO HELPS MAKE IT MORE MANAGEABLE. THIS DESIGN TAKES A SQUARE BLOCK AND BREAKS IT UP INTO A SMALLER, ON-POINT SQUARE AND FOUR SURROUNDING TRIANGLES. THE BLOCK CAN BE DIVIDED IN A MYRIAD OF WAYS, SO TRY TWEAKING THE DESIGN TO SEE WHAT YOU CAN COME UP WITH!

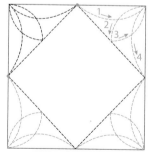

3. Repeat Step 2, filling in each of the "triangles" of the block, working your way around. You will end at the starting point.

VARIATIONS

To fill in larger blocks or to create more dense quilting, you can echo the inside of the square and add a filler. In the example at right, I quilted the on-point square and then used the mitered corners design (page 16) and filled inside with swirls before moving on to Step 2. I'm sure you can see that there are many different possibilities with this design.

When using this design in larger square blocks, try echoing inside the square and filling with swirls.

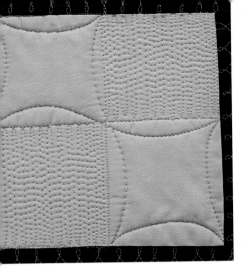

SQUARE 10

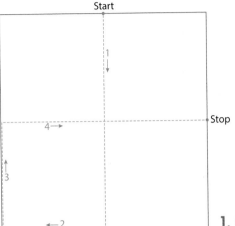

INSTEAD OF TACKLING ONE BIG SQUARE, USE THIS DESIGN TO MAKE FOUR SMALLER SQUARES. BREAKING UP THE LARGER SQUARE IS EASY. FOR THE SMALLER SQUARES, I CHOSE TWO DESIGNS THAT CONTRAST WELL WITH EACH OTHER: CONTINUOUS-CURVE LINES AND DENSE BACK-AND-FORTH LINES. THE CLEAR CONTRAST ENSURES THAT YOUR QUILTING WILL GET NOTICED!

THIS DESIGN WORKS IN BLOCKS OF ALL SIZES, FROM SMALL TO LARGE.

1. Starting from the middle of the top of the block, quilt a vertical line straight down to the opposite side. Travel along the edge, then around the corner to the midpoint of the next side. Quilt a straight line across to the middle of the opposite side. You've divided the block into four convenient sections.

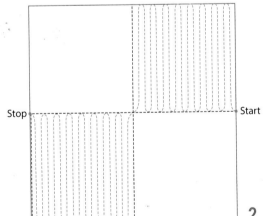

2. Quilt back-and-forth lines, filling in one of the square sections. When the section is filled, cross over the center of the block and continue filling in the square section catty-cornered to the one you just quilted.

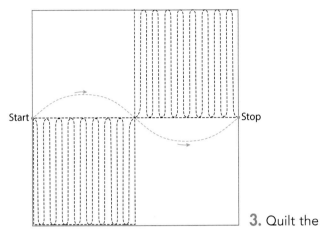

3. Quilt the remaining sections with a continuous-curve design. Start by quilting a curved line to the center of the block. From the center, quilt a curved line into the catty-cornered square.

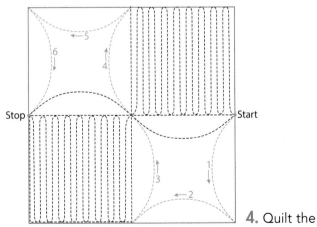

4. Quilt the remaining 3 curves for this square and then resume quilting the curves for the other square, ending at the starting point.

VARIATIONS

Sometimes when I am quilting this design, I like to switch things up just a bit by quilting the back-and-forth lines diagonally instead of horizontally.

You can also quilt this design with diagonal back-and-forth lines.

TRIANGLES

Pieced by Kathy Limpic and quilted by Angela Walters

Whether setting triangles, Flying Geese blocks, or just plain old triangle blocks, triangles are probably my least favorite shape to quilt. Most likely it's because they are less common than their square counterparts and they have all those diagonal lines. But regardless of how much I like or dislike quilting them, I have some go-to favorite designs. I hope by the time you are done with this chapter, you will have added several favorites to your machine-quilting repertoire.

Tips for Quilting Triangles

CONSIDER THE SIZE.
Try keeping the designs more basic in smaller triangles.

BREAK IT UP.
Consider breaking up larger square blocks by quilting two triangle designs. Depending on the quilt pattern, you may also be able to combine smaller triangles to make larger shapes.

USE THE DESIGNS FOR TRIANGULAR SHAPES WITHIN A BLOCK.
If your quilt contains Flying Geese, pinwheels, or actually any block with triangular pieces, you can quilt a design on each triangle. This approach really expands your options, from the simplest half-square triangle to complex kaleidoscope blocks. For strong graphic effect, you can plan the stitching direction in the triangle patches so your quilting creates a larger design.

THINK OF DIFFERENT WAYS TO USE THE TRIANGLE DESIGNS.
Repeat them in a border or use them in the negative space of a quilt. Or, try combining different designs to come up with an original one!

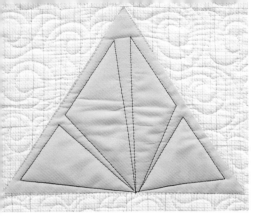

TRIANGLE 1

THIS DESIGN IS PERFECT FOR MEDIUM TO LARGER TRIANGLES BUT DOESN'T FIT IN SMALLER TRIANGLES AS EASILY. IT'S ALSO APPROPRIATE FOR SQUARE-SHAPED BLOCKS.

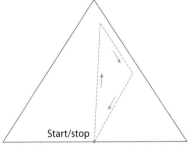

Start/stop

1. Starting from the middle of one side of the triangle, quilt a straight line toward the opposite point, stopping slightly right of center, approximately ¼˝ to ½˝ from the edge of the block. Echo down diagonally about 1˝ and return to the starting point.

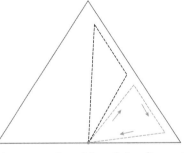

2. Quilt another triangular shape to the side of the first triangle. Return to the starting point.

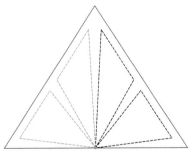

3. Quilt the other side of the triangle the same way.

VARIATIONS

Shifting the design to start from a corner is a seemingly small change, but it changes the appearance noticeably.

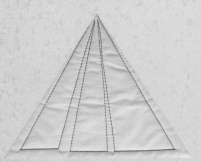

Rotating this design is a quick way to give it a different look.

TRIANGLE 2

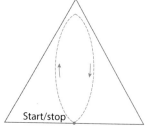

1. Starting from the midpoint of one side, quilt a curved line that comes to a point just shy of the opposite point, and arc back down, returning to the starting point.

I AM A HUGE FAN OF QUILTING FEATHERS, PROBABLY BECAUSE IT TOOK ME A LONG TIME TO LEARN HOW TO STITCH THEM! I LOVE TO USE FEATHERS IN ALL PARTS OF A QUILT. BORDERS, BACKGROUNDS, AND BLOCKS ARE ALL FAIR GAME. TRIANGULAR SHAPES ARE A PERFECT SETTING FOR THIS FEATHER-FUL DESIGN.

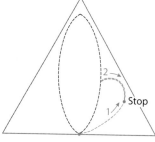

2. Quilt a petal to one side of the middle until it touches. Backtrack along the petal until you are just over the top part of the petal.

TIP

Depending on the size of the triangle block you are quilting, you could use more (or stop at fewer) petals.

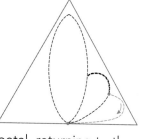

3. From that point, quilt another petal, returning to the starting point.

VARIATIONS

To customize this design, try adding another loop inside the center shape.

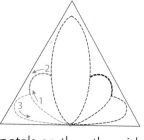

4. Repeat Steps 2 and 3 to quilt petals on the other side of the triangle.

Quilting a loop in the center of the feather is an easy way to extend this design.

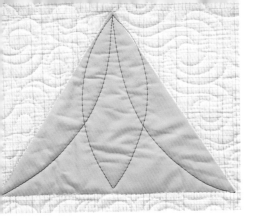

IF YOU COULD LOOK UP "QUICK, EFFICIENT QUILTING DESIGNS" IN THE DICTIONARY, YOU WOULD SEE A PICTURE OF A CONTINUOUS CURVE. QUILTING A GENTLY CURVED LINE FROM POINT TO POINT MAKES FOR A REALLY QUICK AND YET ELEGANT DESIGN FOR QUILT BLOCKS OF ALL SIZES AND SHAPES. I TEND TO USE THIS FOR LARGER QUILT BLOCKS MADE UP OF SMALLER TRIANGULAR PIECES.

TRIANGLE 3

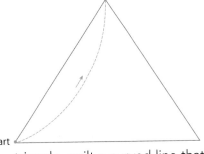

1. From one point of the triangle, quilt a curved line that goes to the next point.

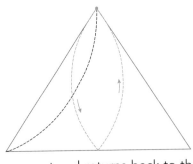

2. Quilt a petal shape that arcs out and returns back to the second point.

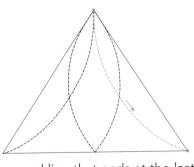

3. Finally, quilt another curved line that ends at the last point of the triangle.

VARIATIONS

If you are quilting a larger triangle or want to stitch a more intricate design, add more curved lines to help fill in the block more evenly.

You could also increase the number of curved lines to create more petals.

TIP

Experiment with this design using other shapes, including squares.

TRIANGLE 4

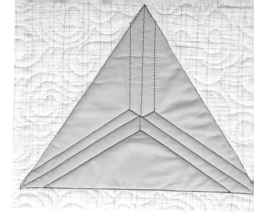

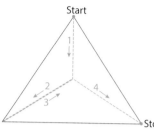

1. From one point of the triangle, quilt a straight line to the center. Quilt a diagonal line to the next point of the triangle and immediately travel back to the center. Quilt a diagonal line down to the third point. You've now formed three inner triangles.

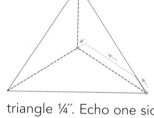

2. Travel along the edge of the triangle ¼˝. Echo one side of an inner triangle, then pivot and quilt a short line to the exact center.

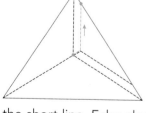

3. From the center, travel back along the short line. Echo along the other side of the inner triangle.

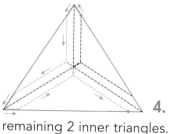

4. Repeat Steps 2 and 3 to echo the remaining 2 inner triangles.

SOMETIMES YOU WILL COME ACROSS A QUILT BLOCK THAT COULD USE A LITTLE MORE QUILTING THAN NORMAL. IF YOU JUST SO HAPPEN TO FACE ONE OF THESE BLOCKS, THIS DESIGN IS FOR YOU. IT'S ESPECIALLY APPEALING WHEN USED IN LARGER TRIANGLES, ALTHOUGH YOU COULD USE IT FOR SMALLER TRIANGLES TOO.

TIP

Using a thread color that blends with the fabric helps keep your stitches looking neat and tidy when traveling.

VARIATIONS

The convenient thing about this quilting design is that the three inner triangles leave space for you to add a meandering design, such as swirls.

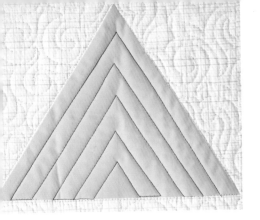

TRIANGLE 5

IF YOU BELIEVE THAT "LESS IS MORE," THEN THIS DESIGN IS PERFECT FOR YOU. SIMPLY ECHOING TWO SIDES OF THE TRIANGULAR SHAPE IS AN EASY WAY TO QUILT TRIANGLES OF ALL SIZES. I ESPECIALLY LIKE TO USE THIS ON THE TRIANGLES IN FLYING GEESE BLOCKS.

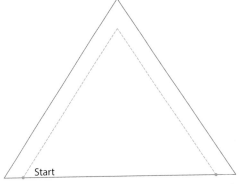

1. Starting ¼˝ from a bottom corner of the triangle, travel along the edge approximately ¼˝ and echo both sides of the triangle.

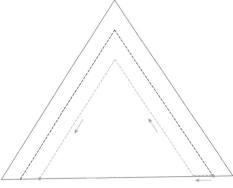

2. Travel ¼˝ toward the inside of the triangle and echo the lines you just quilted.

note Depending on how dense you want the quilting, try spacing the lines closer or farther apart.

VARIATIONS

You don't have to stick with just straight lines. Fill in between random lines with a filler, such as circles, to add extra oomph to your quilt block.

Combine pebbles with the straight lines to give this design a more custom look.

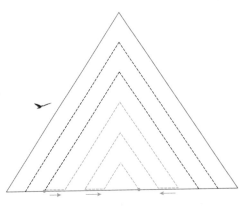

3. Continue quilting lines until the triangle is filled in.

TRIANGLE 6

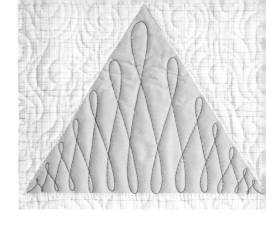

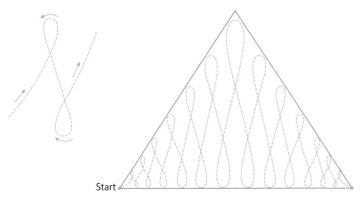

Start

1. Start from one corner and quilt a figure-eight design, filling up the triangle and working toward the opposite corner.

TIP

Use the edges of the block as a guide as you make the figure-eight loops. That will allow the design to stretch and fit perfectly.

ONE OF MY FAVORITE THINGS TO DO IS TO USE CLASSIC QUILTING DESIGNS IN UNEXPECTED WAYS. FOR INSTANCE, I LIKE TO TAKE DESIGNS NORMALLY SEEN IN BORDERS AND SASHINGS, AND USE THEM IN QUILT BLOCKS. THIS FIGURE-EIGHT QUILTING DESIGN IS A GREAT EXAMPLE OF THAT. THE FIGURE-EIGHT DESIGN IS QUICK AND EASY, AND YOU CAN MOLD IT TO FIT IN BLOCKS OF DIFFERENT SHAPES. TRY IT IN TRIANGLES OF ALL SIZES.

VARIATIONS

You could definitely use any design that lends itself to different widths. Instead of a figure-eight design, you can use a dense back-and-forth line.

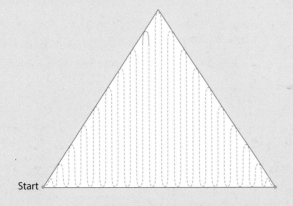

Start

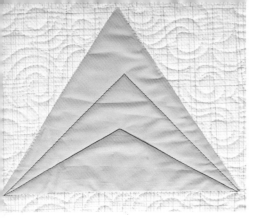

TRIANGLE 7

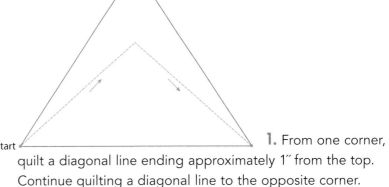

FOR SOME REASON, I HAVE A MUCH HARDER TIME QUILTING DESIGNS IN SMALLER QUILT BLOCKS. I'M SURE IT'S BECAUSE I PREFER QUILTING MORE COMPLEX DESIGNS. THERE ARE TIMES WHEN I NEED A SIMPLER DESIGN, BUT THAT DOESN'T MEAN I'D SETTLE FOR SOMETHING DULL. I STILL NEED IT TO BE INTERESTING. THIS DESIGN IS MOST OFTEN USED IN SMALLER TRIANGLES, ESPECIALLY SETTING TRIANGLES.

Start

1. From one corner, quilt a diagonal line ending approximately 1˝ from the top. Continue quilting a diagonal line to the opposite corner.

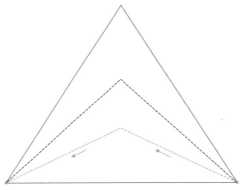

2. Repeat Step 1, except this time stop about 1˝ below the point of the first line you quilted.

VARIATIONS

Even though I demonstrated this design with only two lines, you could always take it a little further by quilting more lines.

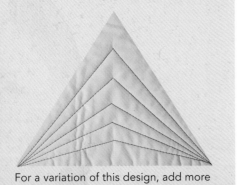

For a variation of this design, add more quilting lines.

TIP

Quilting diagonal lines can be a little tricky. To help keep your lines as straight as possible, try looking ahead of where you are quilting instead of fixating at the needle.

TRIANGLE 8

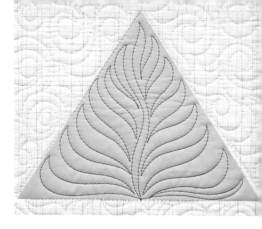

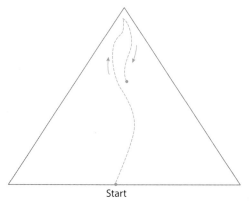

1. Starting from the midpoint of one side, quilt a gentle curve that almost touches the top of the triangle. Quilt a gentle S to form the first side of a petal.

AFTER ALL THE STRAIGHT-LINE DESIGNS IN THIS CHAPTER, I KNEW I HAD TO INCLUDE SOMETHING WITH CURVES. THE POINTY SHAPE OF A TRIANGLE IS PERFECT FOR A FERN QUILTING DESIGN. THIS DESIGN WILL ALLOW YOU TO EASILY AND EVENLY FILL IN TRIANGLES OF ALL WIDTHS.

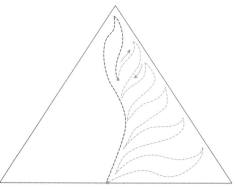

2. Working your way down the spine, quilt petals to fill the area as consistently as possible.

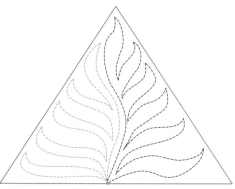

3. Echo up the other side of the spine and quilt petals on the other side of the triangle.

WHAT DID YOU SAY? YOU WANT A MORE COMPLEX QUILTING DESIGN FOR YOUR LARGER TRIANGLE BLOCKS? WELL, LOOK NO FURTHER. THIS DESIGN IS FOR YOU. JUST LIKE THE OTHER DESIGNS IN THIS CHAPTER, YOU DON'T HAVE TO MARK THIS ONE BEFOREHAND. THIS DESIGN IS DEFINITELY FOR MEDIUM TO LARGE BLOCKS; IT OBVIOUSLY WON'T FIT IN SMALLER ONES.

note When quilting this design, the thread can really start to build up at the starting point. Using a thinner thread that blends in with the fabric, such as So Fine #50 by Superior Threads, will help prevent it from being too distracting.

TRIANGLE 9

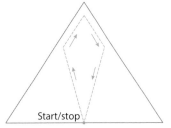

Start/stop

1. Starting from the midpoint of one side of the triangle, quilt a diagonal line, stopping about a third of the way from the top. Echo inside the point of the triangle about ¼˝ until you are on the other side of the triangle. Return to the starting point.

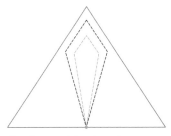

2. If your block is large enough, echo inside the shape you just quilted.

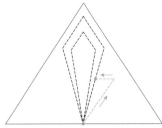

3. To add the sides of the motif, quilt a line going out to the side diagonally and stop about 1˝ from the side of the triangle. Quilt a horizontal line that touches the center of the design.

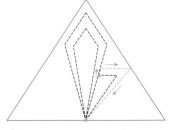

4. Travel up the side of the center motif about ¼˝ and echo outside the shape you just quilted, returning to the starting point.

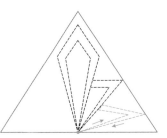

5. Repeat Steps 3 and 4 to add one more section to the side of the motif.

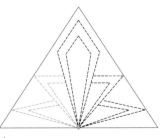

6. Repeat Steps 3–5 to create the other side of the design.

TRIANGLE 10

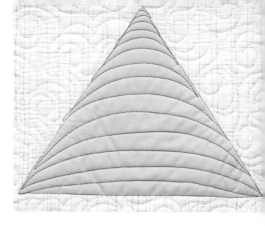

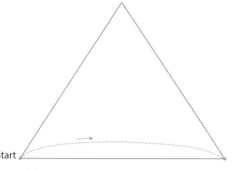

1. Starting from the base of the triangle, quilt a slightly curved line that goes from one point to the other.

WE HAVE ALREADY LOOKED AT DESIGNS WITH CURVED LINES IN TRIANGLES, BUT I WANT TO SHOW YOU JUST ONE MORE. THIS DESIGN TAKES ARC-SHAPED LINES AND STACKS THEM TO GIVE YOUR TRIANGLE BLOCKS A MORE ROUNDED LOOK.

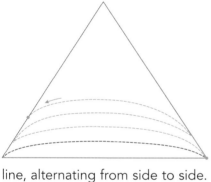

2. Echo the first curved line, alternating from side to side.

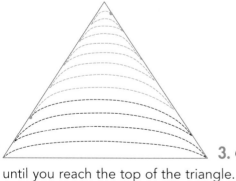

3. Continue quilting arcs until you reach the top of the triangle.

TIP
When quilting the curved lines, make sure to tuck the ends of the curve into the edges of the triangle. This will ensure that your curved lines stay curved and won't flatten.

CIRCLES

Pieced by Kathy Limpic and quilted by Angela Walters

Whether pieced or appliquéd, circles are some of my favorite shapes to quilt. I know I am definitely better at quilting them than piecing them! This chapter will show you several designs to use on circle blocks of all sizes. But before we begin, a few thoughts about quilting circles:

WHAT ABOUT STITCHING IN-THE-DITCH?

I personally like to quilt in the seams around the blocks in a quilt. Even though staying on the curves of a circle can be a bit tricky, I still quilt around them. I love how the quilting sets off the circular shape. But it is not absolutely necessary, so do what works for you!

CHECK OUT OTHER CHAPTERS.

Many of the designs I have created for squares and hexagons can be used in circle-shaped blocks. The reverse is also true. So be sure to check out those chapters if you are stumped on what to quilt in a circle.

WHAT ABOUT APPLIQUÉ?

A question I am very often asked is whether I like to quilt over appliqué. There's a good chance that you will come across circles that are appliquéd, so knowing how to approach them will help make the quilting go smoothly. As with most everything quilting related, this is a matter of personal preference. When I am quilting a quilt with appliqué (of any shape), I try not to quilt over the top of it. However, if the appliqué is large, I will quilt something on it to help stabilize the quilt. When I do that, I tend to keep the designs fairly simple, so as to not distract from the appliqué. But as I said, that is a personal preference. I am only the expert of my opinion; do what works for you!

Ready to start learning some great designs to use on your circle quilt blocks? Let's get started!

CIRCLE 1

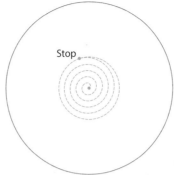

1. Starting in the center of the circle, quilt a spiral until it's about 2˝ from the outside of the circle. Stop so that you are touching the spiral.

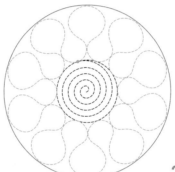

2. Quilt a ribbon candy design, working your way around the spiral and filling in the space as consistently as possible. Return to the starting point.

THIS DESIGN IS GUARANTEED TO HIT THE MARK! USING TWO CONTRASTING QUILTING DESIGNS WILL CERTAINLY DRAW THE EYE TO YOUR BLOCK. IT STARTS AT THE CENTER OF THE BLOCK, WHICH MEANS IT TAKES A LITTLE LONGER, BUT THE RESULT IS DEFINITELY WORTH IT. TRY QUILTING THIS DESIGN IN CIRCLES OF DIFFERENT SIZES.

TIP

I don't worry about finding the exact center when quilting this design; I usually just eyeball it. In my opinion, close enough is good enough!

VARIATIONS

If you want more contrast in your quilting design, try quilting dense back-and-forth lines instead of the ribbon candy design.

Using dense back-and-forth lines instead of the ribbon candy gives this design more dramatic contrast.

CIRCLE 2

1. Quilt a straight line slightly left of center, from the top to the bottom of the circle. Continue quilting a diagonal line to the left side of the circle, and horizontally to the right side.

INSPIRATION FOR QUILTING DESIGNS CAN COME FROM ANYWHERE! THIS PARTICULAR DESIGN IS REMINISCENT OF THE TRADITIONAL CHURN DASH QUILT BLOCK AND IS QUICK AND EASY TO QUILT!

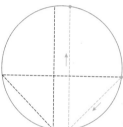

2. Quilt a diagonal line to the bottom of the circle and then straight up to the top of the circle.

note Even though I demonstrate this design in a circle, you could use it for different shapes, such as a rectangle.

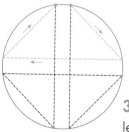

3. Complete the design as shown at left for the top half.

VARIATIONS

You might want to add a little bit of "curve" to this quilting design. Replace the straight diagonal lines with curves, creating a subtle repetition with the circular block shape.

Swap the straight diagonal lines with curves that repeat the block shape and create a different look.

THIS DESIGN SHOWS THAT ECHOING
CAN MAKE ALL THE DIFFERENCE.
THIS FLOWERY-LOOKING DESIGN IS
CENTERED IN THE CIRCLE, BUT DON'T
FEEL COMPELLED TO MARK THE EXACT
POINT. I FIND THAT EYEBALLING IT
IS USUALLY CLOSE ENOUGH.

VARIATIONS

This design works best in
smaller to medium-sized circles,
but you can easily adapt it to fit
larger circles by echoing around
the outside of the petals.
Simply quilt the petal design
and then add echoes to it.

Echo the design to create a different
look or to fill larger circles.

CIRCLE 3

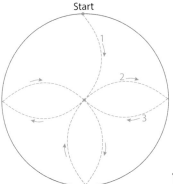

1. From the top of the
circle, quilt a curved line ending at the center of
the circle, forming a half petal. Visualize the circle
divided into quarters and quilt 3 petals, stopping each time at the center of the circle.

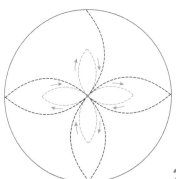

2. Before completing the last
half petal, echo inside the petals you just quilted, including
the half petal.

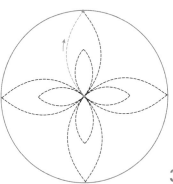

3. Finish the first petal,
returning to the original starting point.

CIRCLE 4

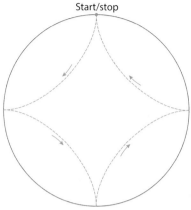

Start/stop

1. Before starting, visualize 4 points that divide the circle into quarters. If you prefer, mark these points for reference. Starting from one point, quilt curves that go from dot to dot, returning to the starting point.

TIP

When quilting curves, look at the ending point instead of focusing right at the needle. It may seem counterintuitive, but I promise it will help ensure that your curves are as even as possible!

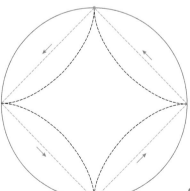

2. Work your way back around the circle using straight lines to connect the points.

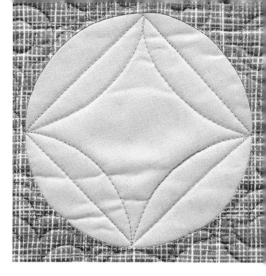

THIS DESIGN PROVES THAT CONTINUOUS-CURVE DESIGNS AREN'T JUST FOR BLOCKS WITH CORNERS! IN THIS DESIGN, WE WILL USE REFERENCE POINTS ON THE CIRCLE TO COMBINE CURVED AND STRAIGHT LINES FOR A MODERN LOOK. THIS DESIGN PERFORMS WELL FOR CIRCLES OF ALL SIZES.

VARIATIONS

If your quilt blocks would benefit from a little more quilting, echo inside the curved lines.

Echo the curved lines for an easy variation.

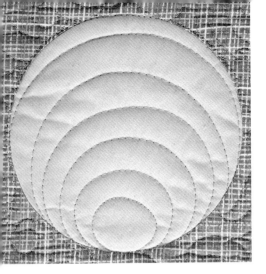

WHEN IS A CIRCLE NOT A CIRCLE?
WHEN YOU USE THE QUILTING TO GIVE
IT AN OFFSET LOOK. ALL IT TAKES IS A
SMALLER CIRCLE AND SEVERAL ECHOES
AROUND IT TO CREATE AN OPTICAL
ILLUSION THAT WOULD BE A FANTASTIC
CHOICE FOR CIRCLES OF ALL SIZES.

VARIATIONS

If your circles need a little more pizazz, no worries! After quilting the first circle in Step 1, fill inside with the free-motion quilting design of your choice. For me, filling it with tiny circles seems like an obvious choice!

Try adding pebbles inside the smallest circle.

CIRCLE 5

Start/stop

1. Starting at the edge of the circle, quilt a small circle that touches the edge, ending where you started. You can make it as large or as small as you would like.

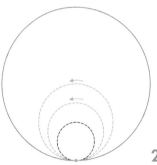

2. Echo around the outside of the circle you just quilted. Make sure the echoed lines are tucked into the edge of the circle block.

note Although I like to quilt my echoed lines about ¼″ apart, you could space them farther apart if you want less dense quilting.

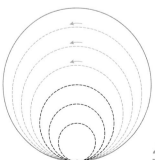

3. Continue echoing until you have filled the whole circle.

CIRCLE 6

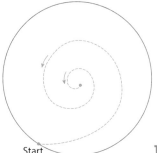

Start

1. Starting from any point on the outside edge of the circle, quilt a spiral inside the circle, ending at the center.

TIP

Try to keep the lines at least 1″ apart. This will ensure that you have room to quilt the petals in the next step.

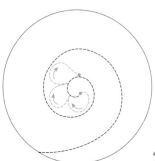

2. From the center of the circle, start adding petals along the spiral. For the petals, imagine that you are quilting a half heart shape.

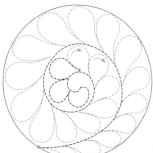

3. Continue adding the petals, filling in the space consistently until you end up where you started.

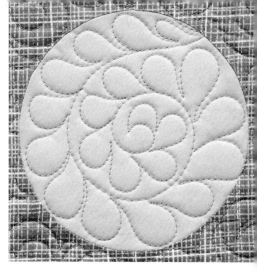

FEATHERS, FEATHERS, FEATHERS—IS THERE ANYTHING BETTER? THIS DESIGN IS A TWIST ON THE CLASSIC QUILTING FEATHER. ALTHOUGH I OFTEN USE THIS DESIGN IN SQUARE BLOCKS, I INCLUDED IT IN THIS CHAPTER TO SHOW THAT IT'S PERFECTLY APPROPRIATE FOR CIRCLES.

VARIATIONS

To quilt a variation of this design, echo inside each petal as you go. This is especially effective for larger circles or for circles where you want more quilting.

Try echoing the petals for a variation of the design.

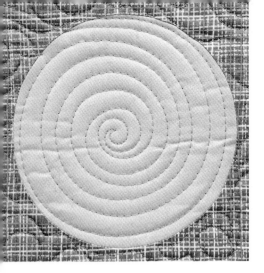

TO ME, THE MOST IMPORTANT THING ABOUT QUILTING IS TO HAVE FUN. AND I THINK QUILTING IS FUN WHEN IT'S EASY AND QUICK; THAT'S EXACTLY WHAT THIS DESIGN IS. THERE'S NOTHING COMPLEX OR INVOLVED ABOUT THIS ONE. I AM SIMPLY TAKING A SPIRAL QUILTING DESIGN AND PLACING IT IN A CIRCLE.

CIRCLE 7

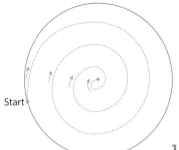

Start

1. Starting from any point on the outside of the circle, quilt a spiral ending in the center of the circle, keeping the lines approximately ½″ apart.

note To help keep the spacing between the lines consistent, I like to use the presser foot as a guide.

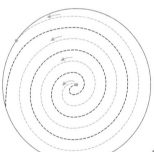

2. Abruptly change direction and echo your way back out, trying to stay an even distance between the lines of the spiral. Continue until you reach the edge of the circle.

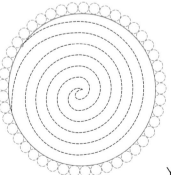

You can extend the quilting outside the block by adding small circles around the perimeter. This detail will add another layer of richness to your quilting.

CIRCLE 8

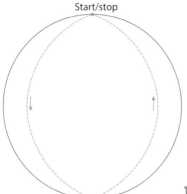

Start/stop

1. Starting from the top of the circle, quilt an arc going to the opposite side of the circle. Quilt another arc back up to the starting point.

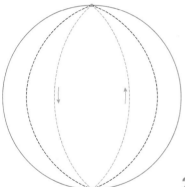

2. Repeat Step 1, echoing inside the arcs you just quilted. Return to the starting point.

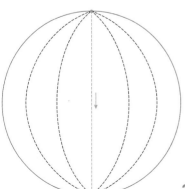

3. As an optional step, you can quilt a straight line down to the bottom of the circle.

THIS IS MY DEFAULT QUILTING DESIGN FOR SMALL CIRCLES. IT'S QUICK AND EASY, BUT MORE INTERESTING THAN JUST STITCHING IN-THE-DITCH.

VARIATIONS

I usually add another design in the center if I want to end up on the other side of the circle. However, instead of a straight line as done in Step 3, you could quilt a different design such as the ribbon candy inside the echoed curves.

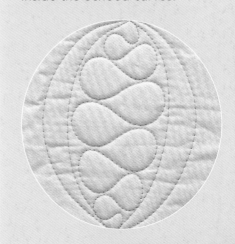

THIS DESIGN STARTS IN THE MIDDLE OF THE CIRCLE, WHICH MEANS IT TAKES A BIT LONGER TO QUILT IT. BUT I THINK THE EFFORT IS WELL WORTH IT!

VARIATIONS

No matter what you are quilting, echoing is a quick and easy way to spice things up. The same is true with this design! Echoing around the outside of the petals not only adds to this design's floral look, but it also helps fill in larger circles.

CIRCLE 9

1. Starting slightly above the center of the circle, quilt a small circle. I usually aim for about 1″ wide.

2. Quilt a line with a smoothly rounded top, stopping when the curve starts to head back down. Backtrack along the curve until you are just over the rounded top.

3. Quilt the curved end of the next petal, heading down toward the center circle. Travel along the center circle just a little; then quilt another petal as you did in Step 2.

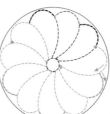

4. Continue until you have filled the entire circle with petals.

CIRCLE 10

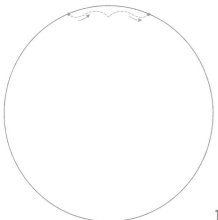

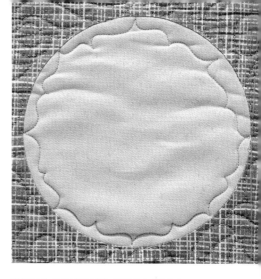

THIS UNDERSTATED LITTLE DESIGN
IS SO VERY VERSATILE! I HAVE ALSO
USED IT IN SQUARES, NEGATIVE
SPACE, AND BORDERS. IT WORKS
WONDERFULLY IN SMALLER CIRCLES.

1. Starting from any point on the edge of the circle, quilt a bracket shape that ends touching the edge.

2. Continue working your way around the circle, repeating the same bracket shape.

TIP

If you are worried that the bracket shapes won't all be the same size, try to imagine the circle divided into equal sections such as fourths or eighths. If you prefer, mark these points for reference.

VARIATIONS

You could also quilt the brackets around the outside of the circle, or you could echo the brackets.

DIAMONDS

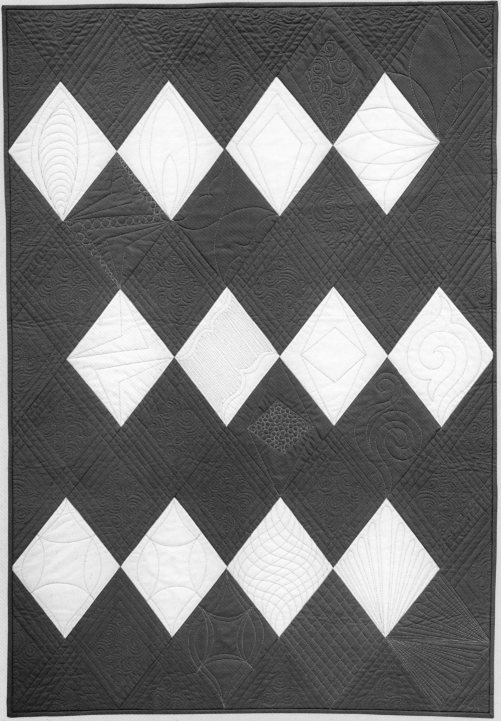

Pieced by Kristi Ryan and quilted by Angela Walters

The diamond-shaped block isn't the most common in the quilting world, but it's always handy to have some favorite go-to designs to use if you come across them. The designs in this chapter range from simple to slightly more complex and, in either case, will make your diamond-shaped blocks look amazing!

How to Get the Most out of This Chapter

> TRY THE DESIGNS IN DIFFERENT-SHAPED BLOCKS.
Since diamond-shaped blocks are similar to squares (think of diamonds as evenly wonky squares), the designs in this chapter can be used in a number of different shapes. Try them in squares or rectangles—I think you will find they are easily adaptable.

> DIVIDE AND CONQUER.
If you can't find a diamond design that will work for your quilt, you can divide the diamond into two triangles and use a design from the Triangles chapter (page 28). Talk about getting more for your money!

> DON'T LET DIAGONAL LINES GET YOU DOWN.
Some of these designs have diagonal lines, which aren't my favorite to quilt. To help make quilting diagonal lines more painless, you can try a few things.

When quilting on a home sewing machine, I like to turn the quilt ever so slightly, so I am quilting a straight line. It may not be possible depending on your machine and the size of the quilt, but if you can maneuver it, it will help keep your lines smoother and more fluid.

If you are quilting on a longarm quilting machine, definitely consider using a ruler. No matter how long the diagonal line is, I always have my trusty ruler on hand.

No matter what kind of machine you use, relax and just enjoy the process. If a diagonal line isn't perfect, don't worry. Just move on to the next one.

> TWEAK IT!
As with all the other designs in the book, try tweaking the diamond designs to create fun variations. If you don't like a particular design, ask yourself what you can change to make it work better for you.

How about we stop chatting and start quilting? Let's dive right into this chapter of quilting designs!

DIAMOND 1

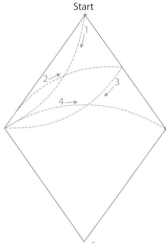

1. Starting from the top of the diamond, quilt a line that curves to the next corner. From there, quilt a curve that goes to the midpoint of the opposite side and curves back. Then quilt a curved line that ends at the opposite point of the block.

NORMALLY, CONTINUOUS-CURVE DESIGNS START AND END AT THE SAME POINT. THIS IS ESPECIALLY HELPFUL WHEN YOU NEED TO GET IN, QUILT THE BLOCK, AND GET OUT AT THE SAME POINT WHERE YOU STARTED. BUT SOMETIMES YOU NEED THE DESIGN TO END AT A POINT OPPOSITE OF WHERE YOU STARTED. I LIKE TO CALL THESE "MOVING ON" DESIGNS.

FOR THIS DESIGN, I TOOK A FAVORITE CONTINUOUS-CURVE DESIGN AND TWEAKED IT JUST A BIT. I HOPE YOU LIKE IT AS MUCH AS I DO!

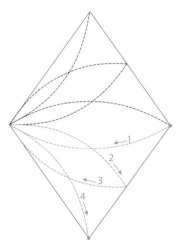

2. Continue quilting the block as shown, ending at the bottom corner of the block.

note Don't worry if the design doesn't land exactly in the middle of the sides. Once the quilt is finished, it won't be noticeable at all!

VARIATIONS

If you want to use this design in smaller blocks or if you want less dense quilting, reduce the number of curved lines. The example at right has only one full petal. Simple and stunning!

DIAMOND 2

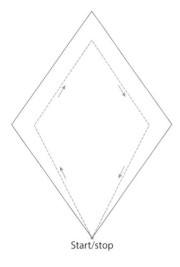

Start/stop

1. Starting from the bottom of the diamond, quilt a diagonal line that stops about 1″ from the next corner of the diamond. Echo along the top 2 sides of the diamond, stopping about 1″ from the third corner. Return to the starting point.

I REALLY DISLIKE HAVING TO MARK QUILTING DESIGNS, SO I LOVE TO FIGURE OUT HOW TO STITCH INTERESTING DESIGNS WITHOUT RESORTING TO MARKING. THIS STRAIGHTFORWARD DESIGN IS A GREAT EXAMPLE. INSTEAD OF MARKING THE DESIGN, YOU WILL USE THE CORNERS OF THE BLOCK AS REFERENCE POINTS. THE END RESULT MAY NOT BE GEOMETRICALLY PERFECT, BUT HEY, CLOSE ENOUGH IS GOOD ENOUGH!

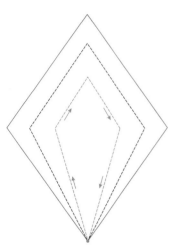

2. Repeat the first step, quilting another diamond shape inside the one you just quilted.

VARIATIONS

This is one of my favorite go-to designs for quilt blocks of all shapes and sizes—it's just that versatile. For example, try it in square- or rectangle-shaped blocks.

When I have a design consisting only of straight lines, I can hardly leave it alone, so I will share this variation that includes a free-motion filler. After Step 2, you can fill inside the diamond with a filler of your choice, such as swirls.

To really draw attention to your quilt block, quilt a variation of this design by adding some free-motion quilting.

SOMETIMES I WANT TO USE DESIGNS WITH SOFTER LINES FOR A CURVIER LOOK. FOR THOSE TIMES, I LIKE TO USE THIS DESIGN. IT'S EASY TO QUILT AND IT LOOKS LIKE PRETTY PETALS. WHAT COULD BE BETTER THAN THAT? THIS IS ALSO ONE OF THOSE DESIGNS THAT STARTS AND STOPS AT THE SAME SPOT, WHICH MEANS I CAN GET IN, GET OUT, AND MOVE ON TO THE NEXT BLOCK.

DIAMOND 3

Start/stop

1. Starting from the bottom of the diamond, quilt a line that curves up to the top of the diamond without actually touching the point, and curve back to the bottom. Try to get the curved portions of the petal as close to the sides as possible, which will help fill the block as much as possible.

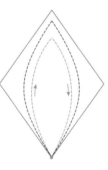

2. Echo inside the petal shape, returning to the starting point. I usually keep the lines about ½˝ apart, but you could make the lines closer or farther apart.

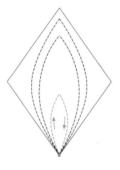

3. Finish the design by quilting a much smaller third petal inside the medium one.

VARIATIONS

For a variation, instead of quilting the smaller petal, you can fill inside the larger petal with a different design. I opted to quilt arcs inside the petal as a variation, but of course, you could use a filler of your choice!

This design is easy to tweak! Simply fill in with a different quilting design.

DIAMOND 4

Start/stop

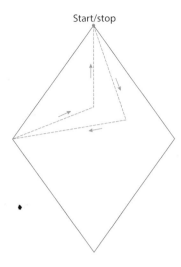

1. Starting from the top of the diamond, quilt a diagonal line, stopping about 1″ from the next corner. Quilt horizontally to the opposite point; then echo inside the shape you just quilted, returning to the starting point.

THIS IS ANOTHER DESIGN THAT USES THE CORNERS OF THE BLOCK AS REFERENCE POINTS. I LOVE THE JAGGED LOOK AND LOVE TO USE IT ON BLOCKS OF ALL SIZES. DON'T LET THE NUMBER OF INSTRUCTION WORDS PUT YOU OFF, BECAUSE THIS ONE IS SIMPLER THAN IT LOOKS: EASIER *DONE* THAN *SAID*!

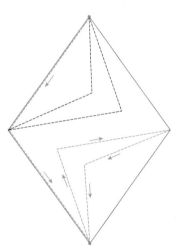

2. Travel along the side of the diamond until you reach the bottom point of the diamond. Quilt the bottom half of the diamond as shown.

TIP

If you need this design to start and end at the same point, you could quilt a line that zigzags between the sections.

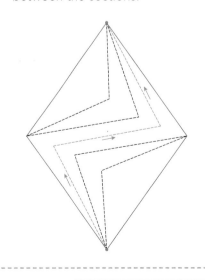

VARIATIONS

Although this geometric quilting design is stunning all on its own, that doesn't mean you can't add to it! You could fill in the space between the quilting designs with pebbles.

Add pebbles between the lines if you want even more quilting.

DIAMOND 5

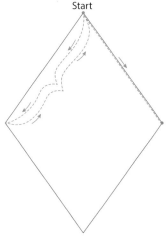

Start

1. From the top of the diamond, quilt a bracket to the next point and echo back to the top. Travel along the side of the diamond to get to the opposite side of the diamond.

SURELY YOU DIDN'T THINK I WAS DONE WITH THE BRACKETS DESIGN? I'VE SAID IT BEFORE AND I WILL SAY IT AGAIN: THIS HANDY DESIGN IS SO VERSATILE. FOR THIS DESIGN, I AM COMBINING IT WITH DENSE BACK-AND-FORTH LINES TO CREATE A STUNNING VISUAL. YOU CAN EASILY MODIFY IT TO FIT QUILT BLOCKS OF ALL SIZES AND SHAPES.

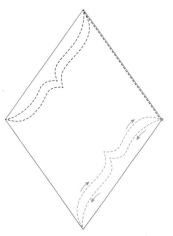

2. Quilt a bracket to the bottom of the diamond and echo back.

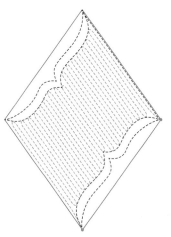

3. Using a dense back-and-forth line, fill in the area between the brackets, working your way to the other side of the diamond.

VARIATIONS

note This design works like a dream in blocks of all shapes, including rectangles.

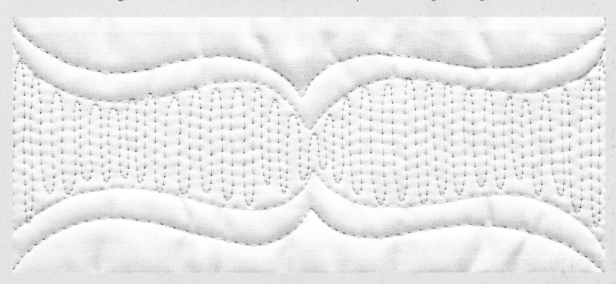

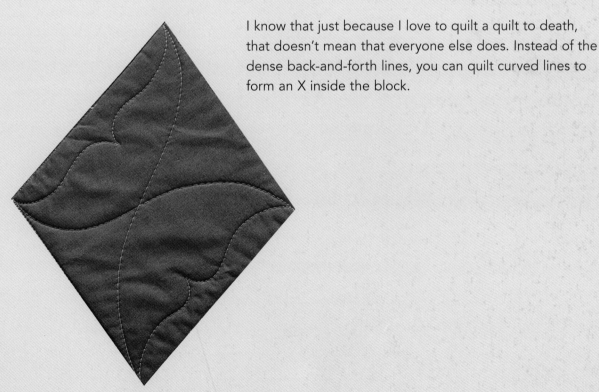

I know that just because I love to quilt a quilt to death, that doesn't mean that everyone else does. Instead of the dense back-and-forth lines, you can quilt curved lines to form an X inside the block.

For less dense quilting, leave out the back-and-forth lines and quilt curved lines to form an X.

DIAMOND 6

AT FIRST GLANCE, THIS DESIGN MIGHT SEEM A LITTLE TRICKY. I PROMISE YOU, IT ISN'T! DON'T LET ITS TRICKY APPEARANCE DISSUADE YOU FROM TRYING IT. ALL WE ARE DOING IS QUILTING STRAIGHT LINES. I KNOW YOU CAN DO IT!

THIS DESIGN CATCHES THE EYE BECAUSE IT'S SO UNEXPECTED. TRY IT IN BLOCKS WHERE YOU REALLY WANT TO DRAW ATTENTION. IT WORKS BEST IN MEDIUM TO LARGE BLOCKS; TRYING TO QUILT THIS IN A SMALLER BLOCK WOULD BE HARD TO FINESSE.

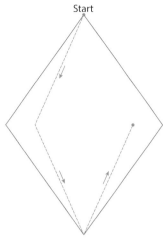

1. Starting from the top of the diamond, quilt a diagonal line ending about 1″ inside the next point. Quilt a diagonal line that touches the bottom of the diamond. Continue up the side of the diamond until you are about 1″ from the next point.

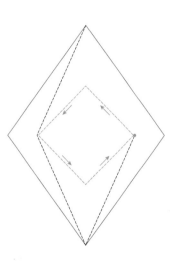

2. From that point, quilt a diagonal line ending about 1″ below the top of the diamond. Quilt a line diagonally until you touch the corner of the lines you quilted in Step 1. Continue quilting to about 1″ above the bottom of the diamond, and return to the starting point of this step.

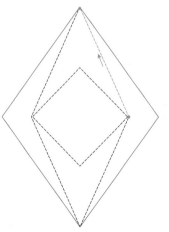

3. To finish the design, quilt a line diagonally up to the top of the diamond.

VARIATIONS

Since this design uses the points of the block as reference points, you can quilt it in several different shapes. For example, in the photo below, I quilted this design in a rectangle.

To dramatically highlight your quilt block, you can quilt a custom variation of this design. Once you finish Step 2, fill inside the square with dense quilting. In the picture below, I used pebbles to fill in the square.

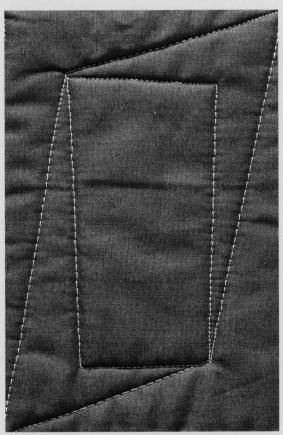

Consider using other shapes, such as rectangles, for this design.

Add a custom look to this design by adding a dense filler such as pebbles.

WHEN WORKING WITH SMALLER BLOCKS, IT'S USUALLY BEST TO KEEP THE QUILTING ON THE SIMPLE SIDE. I LIKE TO USE THIS DESIGN FOR QUILTS WITH A LOT OF SMALLER PIECES. NOT ONLY IS IT QUICK AND EASY, BUT IT ALSO STARTS AND ENDS IN THE SAME SPOT. TALK ABOUT EFFICIENT!

VARIATIONS

If the hooks of this design are throwing you off, omit them and quilt a couple of swirls instead.

DIAMOND 7

TIP

You could also use this design in triangle-shaped blocks. The "hooks" of the design are great for reaching into tight spaces.

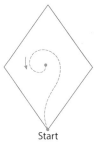

Start

1. From the bottom of the diamond, quilt a swirl in the center of the diamond. Stop in the center of the swirl.

note Make sure to leave space between the edge of the block and the swirl. This will ensure that you have room to complete the design.

2. From the center, add a hook to the swirl by quilting a serpentine line going toward the bottom of the block. From there, partially echo the line you just quilted, stopping about 1″ from the swirl.

3. Echo around the outside of the swirl, coming to a point just below the top of the block. Quilt a small curve to echo the line you just quilted, stopping about 1″ from the swirl.

4. To finish the design, echo around the outside of the swirl, returning to the bottom of the block.

DIAMOND 8

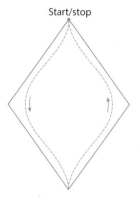

Start/stop

1. Starting from the top of the diamond, quilt a line that curves down to the opposite side of the block and curves back up to the starting point.

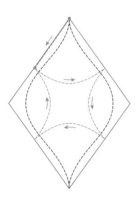

2. Travel along one side of the block until you are approximately at the midpoint. Quilt a concave arc to the other side of the block, aiming for the next midpoint. Repeat 3 more times, working your way around the block and returning to the starting point.

note If you want, you can continue stitching along the seams of the block, returning to the original starting point. I personally like to make sure all the sides of the block are quilted down whenever possible.

OVERLAPPING TWO COMPLEMENTARY QUILTING DESIGNS IS AN EASY WAY TO DEVELOP "NEW" DESIGNS. FOR THIS DESIGN, WE WILL BE QUILTING TWO DIFFERENT CURVY DESIGNS IN DIFFERENT AREAS OF THE BLOCK. I TRULY LOVE CREATING OPPOSITES WITH THE QUILTING—THAT'S WHY I LOVE HOW ONE DESIGN CURVES OUT AND THE OTHER CURVES IN.

THIS ALL-PURPOSE DESIGN WORKS IN DIAMONDS OF ALL SIZES. AND, OF COURSE, YOU CAN USE IT IN BLOCKS OF DIFFERENT SHAPES. I THINK IT JUST MAY BE ONE OF MY NEW FAVORITE DESIGNS!

VARIATIONS

This design is perfect for diamonds of all sizes. However, if you want to use it in a larger block, echoing the lines as you quilt will help fill in the space a little better. To do this, just echo each shape after quilting it.

Echoing the shapes in the design will help fill larger blocks.

THIS DESIGN TAKES THE CLASSIC CROSS-HATCH QUILTING LINES AND GIVES THEM A CURVY LOOK. I THOROUGHLY ENJOY THE OPTICAL ILLUSION VIBE THAT IT HAS. BUT THEN AGAIN, I AM EASILY AMUSED! THE LINES CREATE A STRONG VISUAL IMPACT NOT ONLY IN DIAMOND BLOCKS; YOU COULD ALSO TRY THEM IN SQUARES, RECTANGLES, AND EVEN BORDERS.

DIAMOND 9

1. Starting about ¼″ from the top point of the block, quilt a serpentine line, ending on the opposite side. Travel along the side of the block and echo the first curve, ending about ¼″ below the starting point.

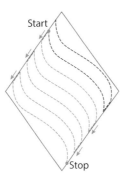

2. Repeat as shown at left, traveling along the sides of the block and quilting serpentine lines until you reach the bottom of the block.

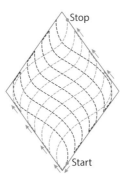

3. Travel along the bottom point of the block until you are on the opposite side of the block. Quilt serpentine lines that diagonally cross the lines already quilted.

VARIATIONS

If you need a more geometric look, you can quilt a straight crosshatch design. Just follow Steps 1–3, quilting straight lines instead of serpentine lines.

To quilt the classic crosshatch design, switch out the serpentine lines for straight lines.

DIAMOND 10

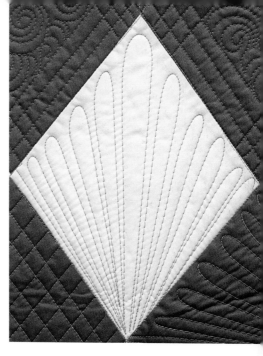

Start/stop

1. Starting from the bottom of the diamond, quilt a line that almost reaches the next corner, curves around, and returns to the starting point.

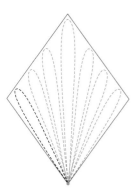

2. Repeat as shown at left, filling in the diamond as much as possible.

BACK-AND-FORTH LINES ARE A STAPLE IN MY QUILTING ARSENAL; I USE THEM ALL THE TIME! THIS DESIGN TAKES BACK-AND-FORTH LINES AND ANCHORS THEM ON ONE POINT OF THE DIAMOND, CREATING A MORE ROUNDED LOOK.

I HAVE USED THIS DESIGN ON BLOCKS OF ALL SIZES SINCE IT IS EASILY ADAPTABLE. I ESPECIALLY LIKE HOW THE LINES OF THE DESIGN LOOK ON CORNER BLOCKS OR ON SASHING. TRY TO SEE HOW MANY DIFFERENT WAYS YOU CAN USE THIS DESIGN ON YOUR QUILTS.

VARIATIONS

Back-and-forth lines are basic, but that doesn't mean you can't use them to make complex-looking designs. For a clever variation, first divide the diamond into 2 smaller triangles and quilt the lines in opposite directions. Fabulous!

Dividing the diamond into 2 triangular areas allows you to use this design in a completely different way but with equally striking results.

HEXAGONS

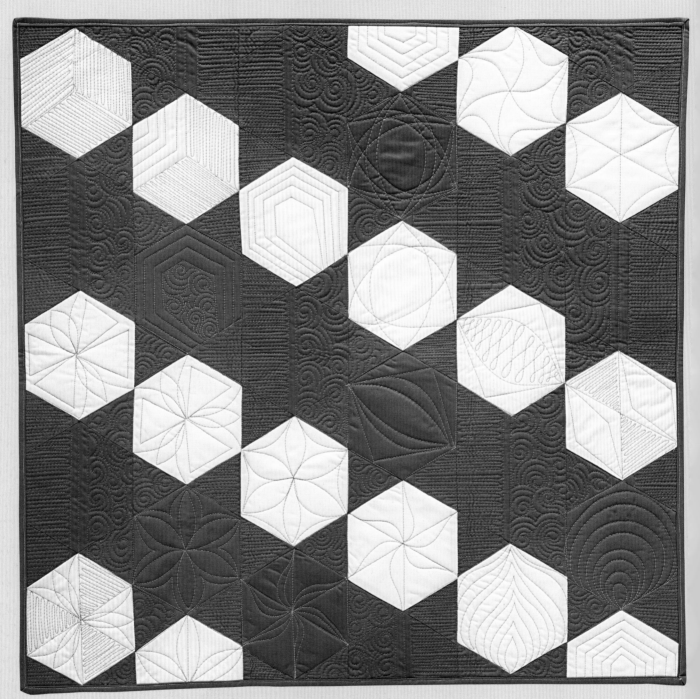

Pieced by Kristi Ryan and quilted by Angela Walters

Hexagons have experienced a resurgence in popularity, so knowing which designs to use can be very helpful! They can be found in quilts ranging from traditional favorites such as Grandma's Flower Garden to random, improvisational modern quilts.

Hexagon blocks can be so entertaining to quilt! Here are a few pointers to get your quilting groove going:

GET TO THE POINT.

I am a huge fan of using the corners (or points) of a block as a guide for the quilting design. So it probably goes without saying that I love the abundance of corners in hexagon-shaped blocks. Choosing quilting designs that go from corner to corner is an easy way to quilt hexagons of all sizes.

WHEN IN DOUBT, CONSIDER CIRCULAR DESIGNS.

A hexagon is fairly similar in shape to a circle (imagine the points morphing) so if at the end of this chapter you still aren't sure what design to use, check out the Circles chapter (see Circles, page 40). Almost all of the designs can easily be adapted to fit in hexagon blocks of all sizes. In fact, some of the designs in the Squares (and Rectangles) chapter would do well in hexagons too!

SEE THE BIGGER PICTURE.

When quilting a quilt that consists of several hexagons, see if you can create secondary designs with the placement of the blocks and the quilting. Try arranging the quilting designs to create flowers or grids. Your imagination is the limit!

Ready to have some hexagonal fun! Let's get started!

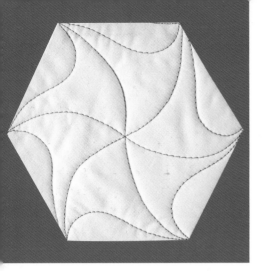

HEXAGON 1

THE POINTS OF A HEXAGON MAKE PERFECT REFERENCE MARKS FOR STITCHING QUILTING DESIGNS. THIS QUILTING DESIGN TAKES FULL ADVANTAGE OF THEM, ALLOWING YOU TO QUILT QUICKLY WITHOUT MARKING!

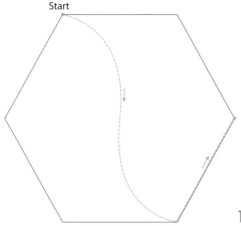

1. From one corner, quilt a serpentine line across to the opposite point. Travel along the edge of the block to the next point.

note This design is fun to quilt in rectangles as well.

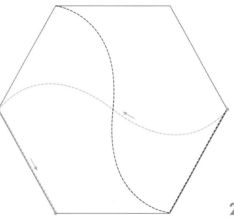

2. Repeat the first step, quilting a serpentine line to the opposite point. Travel to the next point.

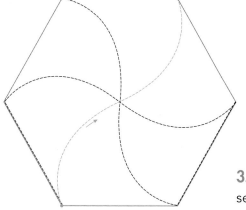

3. Quilt a third serpentine line.

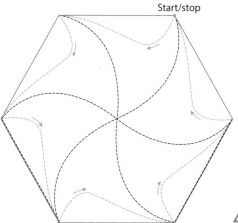

Start/stop

4. From that point, quilt a half heart shape that goes to the next point. To quilt the half heart shape, quilt a line curving out at the beginning and in at the end. Work your way around the block, from point to point, until you arrive at the starting point.

VARIATIONS

To give this quilting design a little twist, straighten it out. Replace the serpentine lines with straight lines and replace the half heart shapes with a more symmetrical arc shape. Either way you quilt it, it's going to look great!

Switch out the serpentine lines with straight lines for a variation of this design.

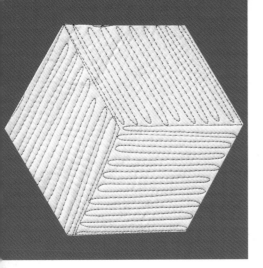

HEXAGON 2

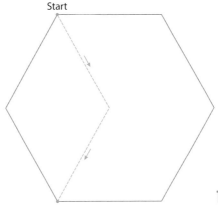

NOTHING MAKES ME HAPPIER THAN QUILTING THAT ADDS TEXTURE. I ESPECIALLY LIKE THIS DESIGN FOR TUMBLING-BLOCK QUILTS, BECAUSE THE DIRECTIONAL LINES DEFINE EACH FACE OF THE TUMBLING BLOCK. THE DENSE BACK-AND-FORTH LINES CREATE TEXTURE THAT INVITES YOU TO RUN YOUR FINGERS OVER IT.

1. From one corner of the hexagon, quilt a line diagonally to the center of the block. Pivot and quilt a straight line to the corner directly below the starting point.

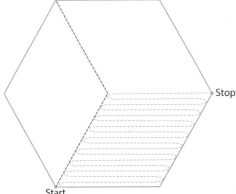

2. Quilt dense lines horizontally from the quilted line to the edge of the block. End so that the last line goes from the center of the block to the corner.

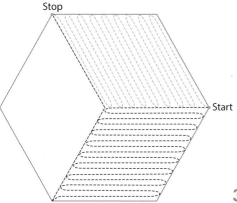

3. From the corner, quilt the same dense back-and-forth lines that you did in Step 2, changing the direction from horizontal to diagonal. End at the top corner of the block.

TIP

Use the edges of the block as a reminder of what direction to quilt the back-and-forth lines.

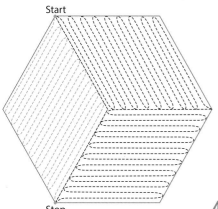

4. Fill in the last section of the block with the back-and-forth lines, making sure the direction of the diagonal lines follows the sides of the block.

To readily move on to the next block, make sure the stitching ends on the bottom corner of the block instead of the center.

VARIATIONS

Quilting all three sections of the block with the same dense quilting provides awesome texture to the quilt. But, if you want to give your block the illusion of depth, quilt one section of the block less densely than the rest. You could also switch out the back-and-forth lines with straight lines that echo the side of the section. The result is quilting that gives your quilt a look of depth.

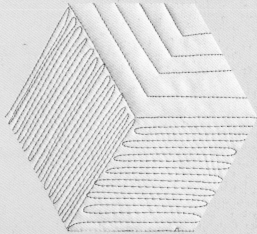

Quilting blocks with designs of different densities will give your block an illusion of depth.

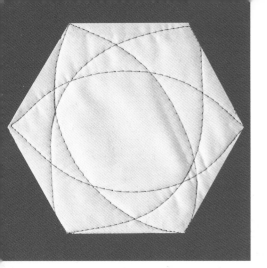

HEXAGON 3

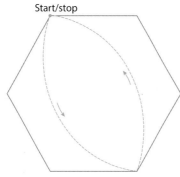

Start/stop

1. From one corner of the block, quilt a curved line ending at the opposite corner. Quilt another curve in the opposite direction, returning to the starting point.

DO YOU REMEMBER SPIROGRAPH? I USED TO LOVE USING THE WHEELS TO REPEAT AND OVERLAP SHAPES TO CREATE COMPLEX DESIGNS. THIS DESIGN IS INSPIRED BY SPIROGRAPH AND USES THE SAME BASIC IDEAS. SINCE YOU ARE USING THE CORNERS AS YOUR REFERENCE POINTS, IT'S EASY *AND* FUN.

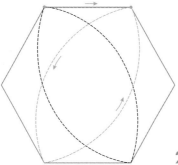

2. Travel along the side of the block until you get to the next point; then repeat Step 1.

note One thing I love about this design is that you stitch in the seams of the block as you go. Now that's multitasking!

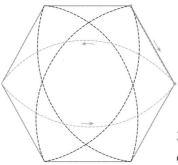

3. Repeat Step 2 to finish the quilting design.

When finished, you can continue traveling along the block to stitch the rest of the seams.

VARIATIONS

TIP

Since the design goes from corner to corner, it's easy to use in blocks of other shapes.

Echoing the design is an easy way to vary any quilting design, especially this one.

If you want a little more of the Spirograph look, you can add quilting in the areas between the curved lines formed by this design and the sides of the hexagon block. Or, you could echo the curves that you quilted.

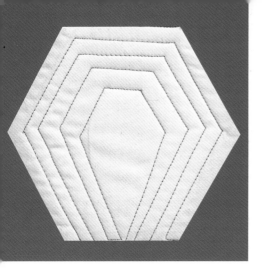

HEXAGON 4

Start

BY SIMPLY ECHOING FIVE OF THE SIX SIDES OF THE BLOCK, THIS DESIGN GIVES THE ILLUSION OF CHANGING THE SHAPE. I LOVE TO USE THIS IN HEXAGONS THAT ARE ARRANGED IN A CIRCLE, SO I CAN FORM A LARGE FLOWER BY VARYING THE DIRECTION OF THE ECHOED LINES.

1. Decide which side of the block you want to serve as the bottom of the quilting design. Start approximately ¼″ inside the bottom corner and echo the other five sides of the hexagon.

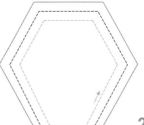

2. Travel along the bottom of the block about ¼″ and echo the lines you quilted in the first step.

VARIATIONS

What good would a quilting design be if you couldn't add some free-motion quilting to it? If you are in the mood for more quilting, you can stop echoing the sides after 3 or 4 lines and fill in the center with a filler design, such as swirls.

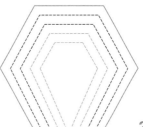

3. Continue traveling along the bottom and echoing the quilting lines until you run out of room at the bottom.

note When you are done quilting inside the quilt block, you can stitch in the seams of the block or just move on to the next block.

Instead of filling the block with straight lines, try filling in the center with swirls.

HEXAGON 5

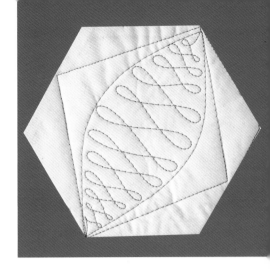

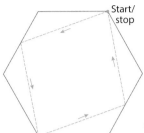

1. Starting at a corner of the hexagon block, quilt a diagonal line to the midpoint of the next side of the block. Quilt diagonally to the bottom corner, then diagonally to the midpoint of the next side. Quilt a fourth line that returns to the starting point.

COMBINING STRAIGHT LINES, CURVED LINES, AND SOME FREE-MOTION QUILTING RESULTS IN A UNIQUE DESIGN. IF YOU ADMIRE MIDCENTURY MODERN DESIGN, YOU WILL LOVE THIS ONE. TRY IT IN MEDIUM AND LARGER BLOCKS.

> **TIP**
>
> I show this design starting at the top right corner of the block, but you can start from any corner.

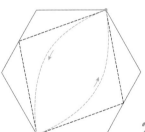

2. Quilt a curved line to the opposite corner and another line curving back to the starting point.

VARIATIONS

This is one of those "moving on" designs. It starts and ends in different places. If you need a design that starts and ends in the same place, instead of quilting a figure-eight design in Step 3, you can echo the curved lines. It fills in the space but also brings you back to where you started.

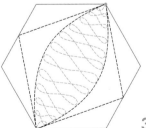

3. Fill inside the curves with a figure-eight design, working your way from the top corner to the bottom corner.

If you aren't sure how to quilt the figure-eight designs, see Triangle 6 (page 35).

Replace the figure-eight design with echoed lines to end where you started.

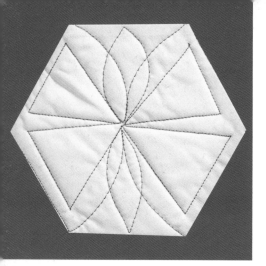

HEXAGON 6

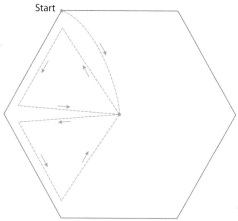

Start

NEXT TIME YOU WANT TO ADD A COMPLEX LOOK TO YOUR QUILT BLOCKS, TRY THIS ONE! IT USES BOTH STRAIGHT AND CURVED LINES, AND DESPITE ITS FANCY LOOK, IT NEEDS NO MARKING.

1. From a corner of the block, quilt a curved line to the center of the block. From the center, quilt 2 triangle shapes that echo the sides of the block without actually touching the edge. Make sure you return to the center.

TIP

It may be helpful to visualize the hexagon block divided into 6 wedges. Quilt the triangles so they fit inside each of the wedges.

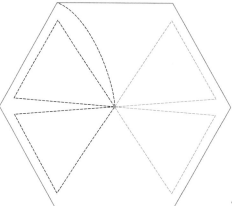

2. From the center, quilt 2 more triangles on the opposite side of the block. Make sure you leave the center bottom wedge of the block unquilted. (We will get to that in the next step.)

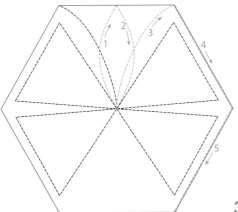

3. Now it's time to quilt the top and bottom section of the block. From the center, quilt a curved line that goes up to the edge, about halfway between the top corners, and returns to the center. Quilt another curved line that goes to the next corner. Travel along 2 sides of the block until you reach a bottom corner.

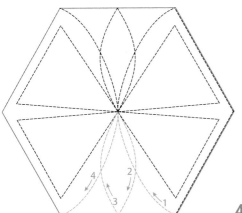

4. From the bottom corner, quilt a line that curves to the center, then out to the middle of the edge of the block and back, and finally curves to the other bottom corner.

VARIATIONS

You can get even more mileage from this design concept and come up with a number of different options. For instance, instead of quilting four triangles and two curved designs, you could make three of each, quilting the curved designs in every other wedge and traveling along the edges of the block as needed.

Use a different layout to give this design another spin.

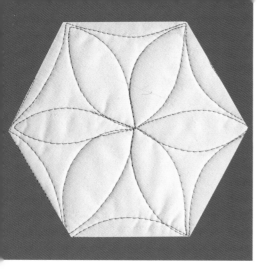

HEXAGON 7

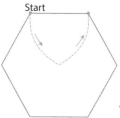

Start

1. Starting from a corner, quilt a line that curves to the center. Quilt a curved line to the next point.

THIS SIMPLE FLOWER DESIGN IS ANYTHING BUT BORING. I USE IT OFTEN IN BLOCKS OF DIFFERENT SHAPES, BUT I ESPECIALLY LIKE IT HERE BECAUSE THE FLOWER LOOKS LIKE IT'S MADE FOR HEXAGONS.

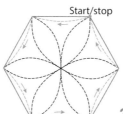

2. Continue working your way around the block, going from a point, to the center, on to the next point, and so on. Stop when you return to the starting point.

TIP

When quilting this design, I just aim for the center. But if you want, you could mark a dot in the center of the block, so it's symmetrical.

Start/stop

3. Quilt curved lines that go from corner to corner until you return to the starting point.

VARIATIONS

I think this design looks a little like a kaleidoscope, but you can change it up a bit for a more floral look. At Step 3, instead of quilting curved lines, echo the sides of the curves. It's a simple twist that completely brings out the floral aspect.

For an easy variation of this design, echo the curved lines instead of quilting the curves in Step 3.

You can also quilt this design in square or rectangle blocks.

HEXAGON 8

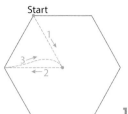

1. From one corner, quilt a diagonal line to the center of the block, then quilt horizontally to the next corner. Quilt a serpentine line back to the center.

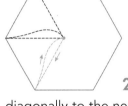

2. From the center, quilt a straight line diagonally to the next corner. Quilt a serpentine line back to the center.

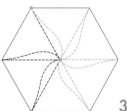

3. Repeat Step 2, going from corner to corner until you reach the original starting point.

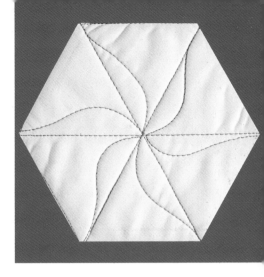

I LIKE THIS SIMPLE DESIGN SO MUCH BECAUSE IT CREATES AN IMAGE OF SPINNING PINWHEELS. USE THIS DESIGN TO ADD A FUN, WHIMSICAL LOOK TO YOUR QUILT.

YOU COULD TRY QUILTING THIS DESIGN IN BLOCKS OF OTHER SHAPES, SUCH AS RECTANGLES.

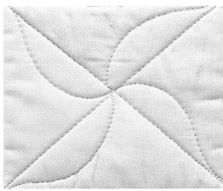

This design works great in rectangles as well.

VARIATIONS

It takes a little more work, but you can tweak this design by echoing the curved lines. To do that, after quilting each section, echo the serpentine curve back to the point. Then travel along the edge of the block to get to the next point.

By the time you're finished, you'll have quilted the block and along the seams.

Echoing the curves takes a little more time, but the result is worth the effort.

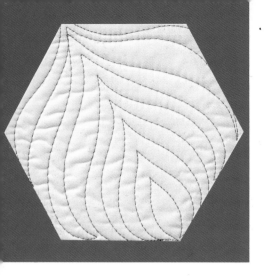

HEXAGON 9

THIS DESIGN IS SIMPLE TO QUILT BUT HAS TONS OF STYLE. IT CAN BE ADAPTED FOR HEXAGONS OF ALL SIZES, FROM SMALL TO LARGE.

Start/stop **1.** Starting from a corner of the block, quilt a small teardrop shape that tapers to a point and returns to the starting point.

TIP

To help keep your design mostly symmetrical, make sure the point of your teardrop is pointing toward the opposite corner.

2. Echo the teardrop again and again until you fill the block as much as possible. Don't worry if the echoed lines are exactly the same. The most important thing is that you fill the space as consistently as possible.

VARIATIONS

Instead of quilting your teardrop with a point, you can round off the end for a whole new look. This will soften the look and give the block a smoother, rounded design.

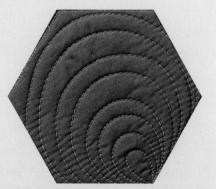

Instead of quilting the teardrop with a point, a rounded end will give you a totally different look.

HEXAGON 10

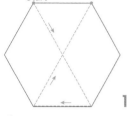

Start

1. Quilt a straight line from one corner to the opposite corner. Travel along the side of the hexagon to the next corner. Quilt a line to the opposite corner.

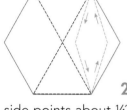

2. From that point quilt a diamond that has side points about ¼˝ from the edge, but touching the corner on the bottom. End at the same point you started.

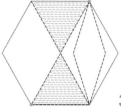

3. Fill in the triangle sections with back-and-forth lines. Start at the top of the block and work your way to the bottom, crossing over the center point. End at the bottom of the unquilted diamond section.

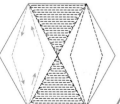

4. Quilt another diamond, as you did in Step 2, but touching the top corner. You should end at the opposite side from the original starting point.

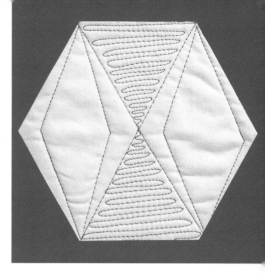

THIS DESIGN HAS EVERYTHING I LOOK FOR IN A QUILTING DESIGN: A COMPLEX LOOK, NO MARKING, AND IT ENDS ON THE OPPOSITE SIDE FROM WHERE YOU START.

VARIATIONS

For a completely different look, you can first divide the block into six triangles and use two different designs that will give you good contrast. This design combines back-and-forth lines with one of the triangle designs (Triangle 3, page 32).

section 2:
NEGATIVE SPACE

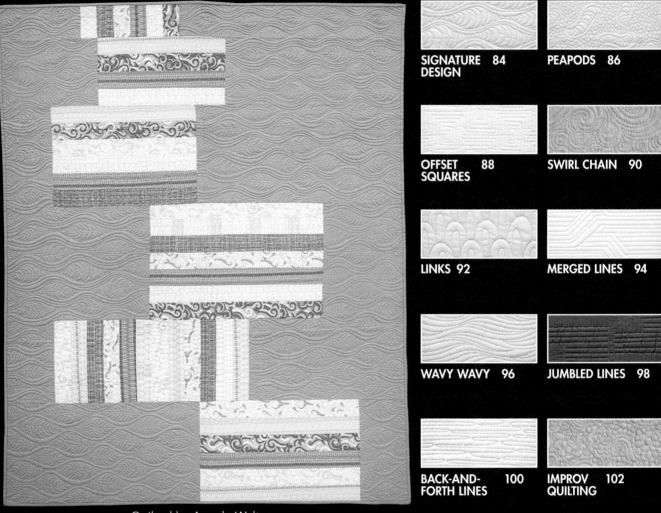

Quilted by Angela Walters

The negative space, or the background, of a quilt is my favorite part of the quilt. The designs you use in this area can expertly enhance and transform your quilt into something exciting! In this section, I share some of my favorite quilting designs to use in the negative space of a quilt.

Since the negative space of a quilt can be any shape or size, I use the term "quilting area" to represent it. The quilting area can be anything from the block background to the whole quilt.

Tips for Quilting Negative Space

> DECIDE HOW MUCH YOU WANT THE QUILTING TO SHOW.

I almost always use thread that blends in with the quilt top; I don't want the quilting to take away from the quilt! The examples in this section are quilted with a contrasting thread color so that the stitches will show up in the photographs. You may have noticed that modern quilters tend to match the thread color to the fabric, but this is your design decision!

> TRY USING THE DESIGNS IN DIFFERENT WAYS.

The designs in this section need not be relegated to the background only! Most of them would be great allover designs or can be adapted to fit into larger blocks or borders.

> PLAY AROUND.

You don't have to quilt the designs exactly how I show you—give them your own twist.

Okay! Enough talking; let's get to the quilting!

SIGNATURE DESIGN

Start

1. Starting at the top of the negative space, quilt a gently waving line to the opposite edge of the quilting area. Travel along the edge approximately ½˝ and echo the first line. Repeat one more time until you have 3 wavy lines.

I LOVE QUILTING DESIGNS THAT ARE FAST, FUN, AND REQUIRE NO MARKING. THAT INCLUDES THIS SIGNATURE DESIGN! NOT ONLY DOES IT ADD MOVEMENT TO YOUR QUILT, BUT IT ADDS A BIT OF CONTRAST WITH THE VERTICAL AND HORIZONTAL LINES. I NORMALLY USE THIS DESIGN IN LARGER AREAS OF NEGATIVE SPACE, BUT IT CAN ALSO GO IN LARGER BLOCKS OR BE USED AS AN ALLOVER DESIGN. NO MATTER HOW YOU USE IT, I'M SURE YOU ARE GOING TO LOVE IT!

note I happen to love the number 3, which is why I chose 3 wavy lines, but you could add more or fewer lines.

2. Travel down the edge of the quilting area a few inches and quilt a wavy line that is a reflection of the wavy line above.

note Don't stress out if it isn't a perfect reflection; close enough is good enough.

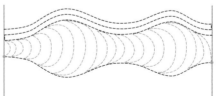

3. Fill in the space between the wave you just quilted and the top set of wavy lines with curved lines, working your way across the area.

TIP

For some help on quilting these curved lines, see one of the triangle designs (Triangle 10, page 39). It looks different there, but the quilting technique is the same!

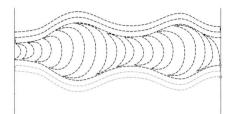

4. Echo the wavy line twice.

TIP

Traveling along the edge of the quilting area will help make sure that wavy lines stay somewhat horizontal.

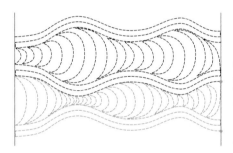

Repeat as shown at left, working your way down and filling in the negative space completely.

A FEW POINTERS

- When quilting the wavy lines, don't quilt them *too* wavy. It will be much easier to quilt if you have gently curving lines.

- Don't stress if it isn't perfect; when the whole area is quilted, it will look great. Also, using thread that blends will hide any imperfections.

VARIATIONS

Try quilting different variations of this design. There are so many different ways you can tweak it! Try quilting the curved lines in opposite directions.

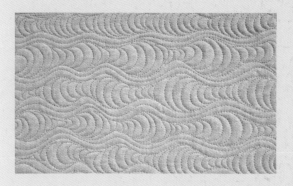

Or, try a different filler design between the wavy lines. The figure-eight or ribbon candy designs are great alternatives.

Quilting the figure-eight quilting design between the wavy lines will give this design a different look.

Try the ribbon candy quilting design between the wavy lines.

PEAPODS

SOMETIMES THE EASIEST WAY TO
COME UP WITH A QUILTING DESIGN
IS TO COMBINE SOME OF YOUR
FAVORITE DESIGNS. PEAPODS DOES
THAT BY COMBINING PEBBLES AND
SERPENTINE LINES. THIS DESIGN IS
FANTASTIC BECAUSE THE QUILTING
CAN BE VERY SMALL AND DENSE OR
LARGE AND AIRY. IT WORKS WELL IN
SMALLER BACKGROUND AREAS OF QUILTS
AND IN LARGER NEGATIVE SPACE.

Start/stop

1. Start by quilting a gentle serpentine line that goes out and echoes back to a point.

2. Echo the sides of the shape, touching the end point and returning to the starting point.

3. Fill inside the peapod shape with a filler. For this example I filled the pod with arcs. End at the opposite point.

4. Fill around the peapod with pebbles.

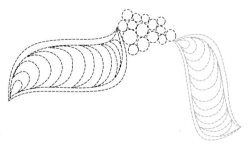

5. Once you have covered enough space, quilt another peapod.

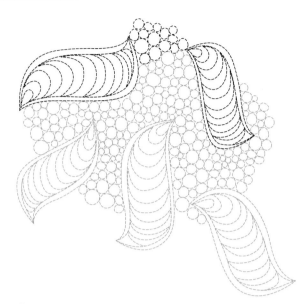

6. Continue quilting pods and your filler quilting design until the area is filled.

TIP

Since the peapods are larger than the pebbles, quilt peapods first and then fill around them with the pebbles.

VARIATIONS

■ **Try switching up the filler design.**
To put your own twist on this design, you could use a different filler, such as swirls. In this variation, I also omitted the filler inside the pods.

■ **Keep the fillers the same.**
If you want the pods to blend in a little more, use the same design inside the pods that you use in the filler.

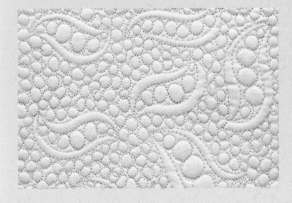

■ Try quilting more pods than the filler quilting for a more complex design.

■ Just remember scale! You can make the design as big or small as you want.

WANT A MORE GEOMETRIC LOOK FOR YOUR QUILTS? THIS DESIGN IS FOR YOU! IT'S A SPIN ON THE SQUARE CHAIN QUILTING DESIGN (PAGE 122), AND THE ONLY DIFFERENCE IS THE LAYOUT OF THE SQUARES. IT'S BEST FOR LARGER AREAS OF NEGATIVE SPACE AND IS EASY TO QUILT. YOU CAN MAKE THE OFFSET SQUARES AS SMALL OR AS LARGE AS YOU WANT.

OFFSET SQUARES

Before starting, let's talk about the square we will be using. Starting from one side, quilt the outside of a box and keep echoing inside until you get to the center. From the center, go across the previously quilted lines so that you'll be in position to quilt the next square.

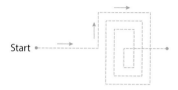

Now let's learn how to offset the squares and give them a neat, tailored-to-fit look.

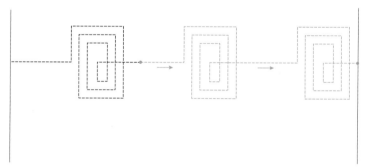

1. Working your way across the quilting area, quilt the squares with spaces in between. Try to keep these spaces roughly the same size as the outermost square.

note Don't measure the boxes beforehand; just eyeball it! Even if they aren't all the same size, the squares will still look great!

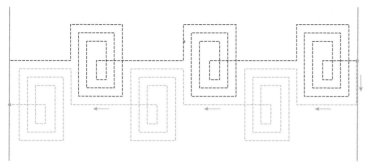

MORE THOUGHTS ...

- If you can't get the spacing quite right, just go with the wonky look.

- Don't worry about the ruler! The lines are short enough that you can get them straight without one.

2. Travel down the edge of the quilting area until you are about ½″ below the bottom of the last square. Work back across the quilting area, offsetting this row of squares to fit into the spaces you left as you quilted the previous row.

3. Continue until the whole area is filled.

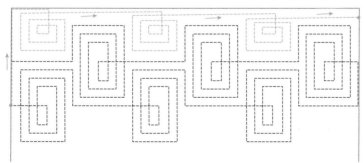

4. When quilting the top and bottom of the quilting area, quilt smaller blocks to fill in the spaces.

SWIRL CHAIN

I AM A SWIRL GIRL AT HEART. TO ME, SWIRLS ARE THE ULTIMATE QUILTING DESIGN. YOU CAN USE THEM IN SO MANY DIFFERENT WAYS AND IN SO MANY AREAS OF THE QUILT. THE SWIRL CHAIN TAKES THE BASIC SWIRL AND PUMPS IT UP A NOTCH. THIS DESIGN LOOKS ANYTHING BUT BASIC AND IS PERFECT FOR FILLING LARGE AREAS OF NEGATIVE SPACE.

note Don't be afraid to try out this design! It's basically just quilting elongated swirls in a row.

Start

1. Starting from the edge of the quilting area, quilt an elongated swirl and echo back to the edge.

2. Travel up the edge about ¼˝, echo *outside* the swirl from Step 1, and echo back to return to the edge again.

3. Travel up the edge about ¼˝ and quilt an elongated swirl that goes out and above the one you quilted in Steps 1 and 2. Return to the edge.

note To help the swirls fit together better, have them point in opposite directions.

4. Travel up the edge about ¼˝ and then echo *around* the swirl from Step 3 so that you are pausing at the point where the 2 swirls meet.

5. Quilt a teardrop shape and echo it. This is an optional step; you could omit the teardrop if you would like.

6. Quilt the next swirl so it goes under the previous swirl. Echo the previous swirl partly, and then create another swirl, ending at the point where the 2 swirls meet.

7. Add a teardrop and quilt the next swirl as you did in Steps 5 and 6.

8. Continue quilting the swirls until you reach the other side of the quilting area.

TIP

When quilting this design, if you find yourself on the wrong side of the swirl, just echo around it until you get to the desired side. By the time you fill in around the design, you won't even notice the extra lines!

QUILTING THE SWIRL CHAIN IN NEGATIVE SPACE

When using this quilting design in the negative space of your quilt, you can quilt it in a few different ways.

- Quilt the swirl chain design in rows and fill in between them with a filler such as swirls. This one adds movement to your quilt but without all the attention going to the swirl chain.

To use the swirl chain design in negative space, quilt them in rows and fill in between with swirls.

- Or, if you want the swirl chains to be much more noticeable, try using a smaller filler such as pebbles.

Fill in between rows of the swirl chain with pebbles to really make the swirl chain stand out.

- Instead of quilting them in rows, you can use the same components of the swirl chain as an allover design. To do so, quilt the elongated swirls in various directions.

Use the swirl chain as an allover design.

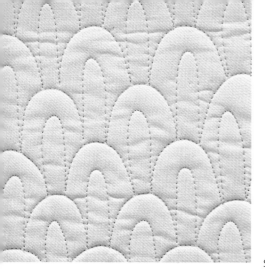

ALTHOUGH IT MIGHT NOT BE OBVIOUS AT FIRST, THIS DESIGN IS ACTUALLY A VARIATION OF THE CLASSIC CLAM-SHELL QUILTING DESIGN. IT IS MADE UP OF TWO BASIC SHAPES AND IS FAST AND EASY TO QUILT. THIS DESIGN IS PRESENTED HERE IN THE NEGATIVE SPACE SECTION OF THE BOOK, BUT IT COULD HAVE JUST AS EASILY FIT IN ANY OF THE OTHER CHAPTERS. IT WORKS IN BLOCKS, BORDERS, OR EVEN AS AN ALLOVER QUILTING DESIGN.

LINKS

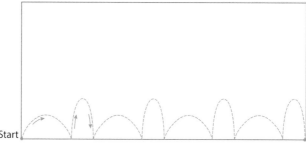

1. Starting at the bottom of the quilting area, quilt a row of arcs. Alternate between short, wide arcs and tall, skinny arcs. As a general guide, the shorter ones should be about twice as wide and half as tall. End when you get to the edge of the quilting area.

note Don't worry about making them perfect. As long as the quilting area is filled in, it will look great!

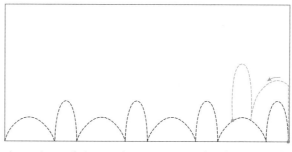

2. Travel up the edge of the quilting area and echo over the top of the skinny arc. Then quilt a skinny arc centered over the wider arc.

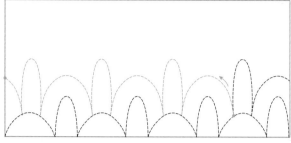

3. Work your way across the quilting area, echoing over the skinny arcs and quilting skinny arcs above the wider arcs. Make sure that the skinny arcs that you quilt on this row are taller than the echoed lines.

TIP

Change up the size to quilt quicker! Making the design larger means that you can quilt more, faster.

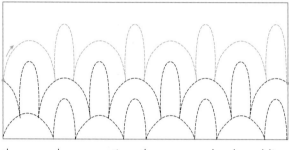

4. Continue quilting the rows by repeating the arcs and echoed lines.

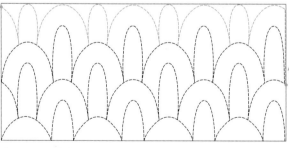

5. When you reach the top of the quilting area, make the skinny arcs short enough to fill in the top completely.

MERGED LINES

WHO KNEW THAT ECHOING STRAIGHT LINES WOULD LOOK SO INTERESTING? THIS DESIGN ADDS A SIMPLE BUT GROOVY LOOK TO YOUR QUILT.

THIS ONE WORKS SPECTACULARLY IN ALL SIZES OF NEGATIVE SPACE OR AS AN ALLOVER DESIGN. YOU MAY BE TEMPTED TO GET OUT THE RULER, BUT I DON'T THINK YOU WILL NEED IT. I QUILT THIS DESIGN WITHOUT A RULER, AND EVEN THOUGH IT ISN'T PERFECT, THE TECHNO VIBE MAKES THE "WIRES" LOOKS GREAT!

1. Start a few inches from the top of the quilting area and quilt a horizontal line toward the opposite side. At a random point, quilt a diagonal line at about 45° and then continue quilting horizontally until you reach the other side.

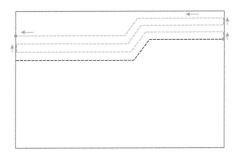

2. Before quilting the rest of the quilting area, fill in above the line, by echoing the first line. For this design, I normally echo about ½˝ apart.

note The first line of this design starts below the top of the quilting area, so you have enough space.

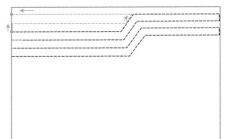

3. You can also echo only a portion of the line. For instance, instead of echoing the diagonal portion of the line, echo just the horizontal part. Travel along the previously quilted diagonal line and return to the edge.

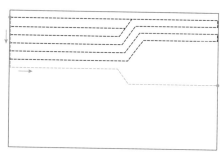

4. Once the top of the area is filled, it's time to quilt the line that will set off the next portion. Travel along the edge so that you are about ½˝ below the first line, and quilt another horizontal line, randomly going down at an angle and then continuing horizontally until you reach the edge.

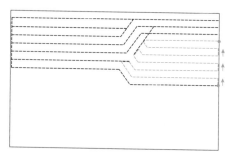

5. Fill in the area between the 2 lines by echoing. Be sure to travel along the edge of the quilting area or previously quilted lines, as shown.

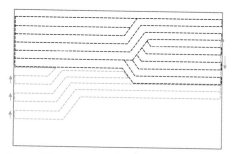

6. After you have filled in the area, travel along the edge of the quilting area and repeat the technique in Steps 1–5.

7. Continue until the quilting area is completely filled.

VARIATIONS

This design is so cool exactly as it is, but if you want something a little different, try quilting an easy variation. Instead of echoing the lines that set off this design, try filling the space with a free-motion quilting design, such as swirls.

Create a variation of this design by leaving out some of the echoed lines and quilting a free-motion quilting design, such as swirls.

I am always looking for ways to make designs look fresh—designs that look a little different from anything I've quilted before. If you want to switch things up as well, you can vary the spacing between the lines or place some pebbles between the lines. The only limit is your imagination!

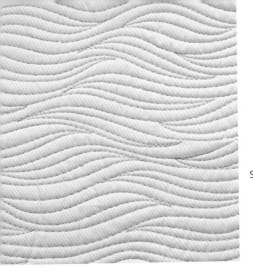

WAVY WAVY

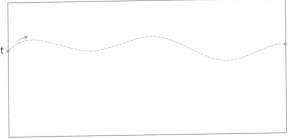

1. Starting a few inches below the top of the quilting area, quilt a gently waving line from one side to the other.

note Starting the design a small distance from the top of the quilting area allows you to get a wavy line on which to build the rest of the design.

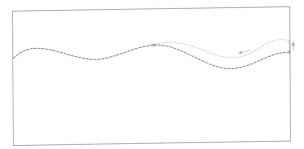

2. Travel up the edge of the quilting area about ½˝. Quilt a wavy line that echoes the first wavy line. At a random point while echoing, run into the line below.

note When you run into the line below, you want the lines to look as if they are merging.

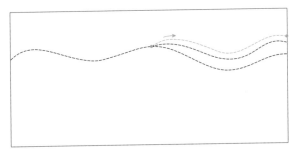

3. Quilt a line echoing back the opposite direction, returning to the edge.

WAVY WAVY SHOWS THAT A SIMPLE DESIGN CAN ADD MOVEMENT AND TEXTURE TO YOUR QUILT. IT'S JUST AN ADDED BONUS THAT IT'S SO EASY TO QUILT. THIS DESIGN IS PERFECT FOR MEDIUM TO LARGE AREAS OF NEGATIVE SPACE OR AS AN ALLOVER QUILTING DESIGN.

note The instructions are just to teach you the technique. When you are quilting this design, you will find your own rhythm.

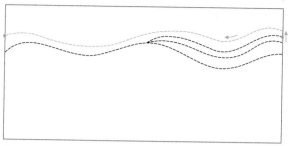

4. Travel up the edge of the quilting area and then echo across to the other edge of the quilting area. Traveling along the edge ensures that your lines will stay somewhat horizontal.

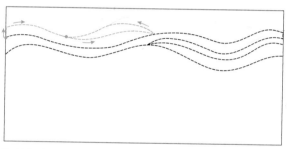

5. Work your way back across the quilt, running into the line below.

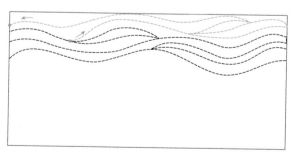

6. Repeat the technique in Steps 1–5, filling in the area.

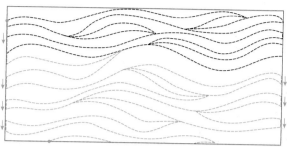

7. Travel down along the edge until you are about ½˝ below the first line (from Step 1). Repeat the technique in Steps 1–6 to fill in the quilting area.

TIP

You can add more movement with this design by running into lines more often.

JUMBLED LINES

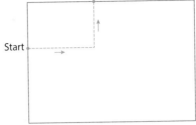

1. Starting from the side of the quilting area, quilt 2 sides of a rectangle.

I LIKE QUILTING DESIGNS THAT INCORPORATE STRAIGHT LINES; WHAT I DON'T LIKE IS QUILTING LONG STRAIGHT LINES OVER AND OVER AGAIN. THIS DESIGN HELPS KEEP ME FROM GETTING BORED! ALTERNATING THE DIRECTION OF THE LINES ADDS A MORE COMPLEX LOOK AND IS ACTUALLY EASY. NO MARKING INVOLVED!

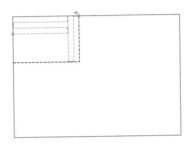

2. Begin filling in the rectangle, alternating between horizontal and vertical lines. Travel along the previously quilted lines.

WHEN QUILTING THIS DESIGN, YOU ARE BASICALLY DIVIDING UP THE QUILTING AREAS INTO SMALLER SQUARES AND FILLING THEM IN.

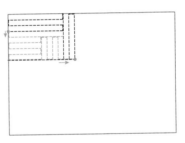

3. Continue until the section is filled. End so that you are at a corner of the rectangle.

TIP

If you get stuck, no worries! Just travel along a line of quilting to get where you need to be.

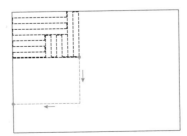

4. Quilt the sides of another rectangle that touches the first one that you quilted.

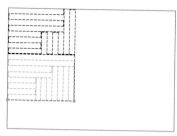

5. Fill in the rectangle by alternating between horizontal and vertical lines, as you did in Step 2.

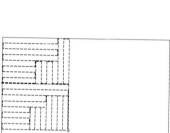

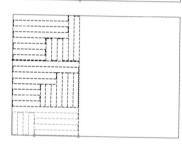

6. When you get to the bottom of the quilting area, you may need to quilt only one line to create the next section.

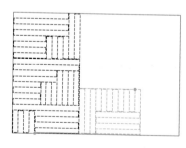

7. Travel along the edge of the quilting area; quilt another rectangle and fill in with lines.

8. Continue until the quilting area is completely filled.

TIPS FOR QUILTING STRAIGHT LINES

- If using a longarm quilting machine, you may want to use a ruler. But I find that if I am quilting shorter lines, I can usually freehand it.

- Using a matching color of thread will help cover any bumps and wobbles.

- Above all, don't stress. Tensing up won't help you at all!

VARIATIONS

To put a fun twist on this design, try combining straight and wavy lines. Use one type of line for the vertical lines and the other for the horizontal lines.

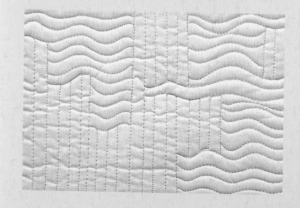

BACK-AND-FORTH LINES

Start

I LOVE THE LOOK OF MATCHSTICK QUILTING: LONG, DENSELY QUILTED LINES OVER THE WHOLE QUILT. THIS DESIGN HAS THE SAME IDEA, BUT THE DIFFERENCE IS THAT WE ARE GOING TO BREAK UP THE DESIGN INTO COLUMNS. THIS CAN MAKE THE QUILTING MORE MANAGEABLE WHEN USING A HOME SEWING MACHINE. I ALSO LOVE HOW THE LITTLE BITS OF UNQUILTED AREA BETWEEN THE COLUMNS GIVE THE QUILT A DISTINCT TEXTURE.

THIS SCALABLE DESIGN CAN BE QUILTED AS SMALL OR AS LARGE AS YOU LIKE. TRY IT IN SMALL AREAS OF NEGATIVE SPACE OR AS A QUICK WAY TO FILL UP LARGER AREAS OF NEGATIVE SPACE. USE THE BACK-AND-FORTH LINES AROUND APPLIQUÉD BLOCKS OR QUILTING MOTIFS TO MAKE THEM POP! AS YOU CAN SEE, THERE ARE SO MANY DIFFERENT WAYS TO USE IT!

1. Starting in a corner of the quilting area, quilt a column of back-and-forth lines that almost touch the edge but are varying widths. Work your way to the bottom of the quilting area.

note Varying the widths of the lines will help the quilting fit together without making the sections so obvious.

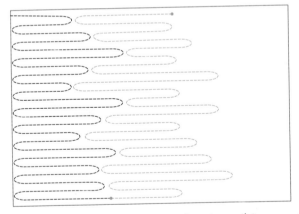

2. At the bottom of the quilting area, begin quilting another column of back-and-forth lines, working your way back up the quilt. Make each of the lines varying widths, but make the lines on one side close to the lines of the previous column.

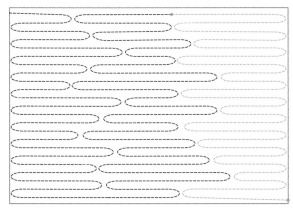

3. Depending on the size of your quilting area, continue quilting columns of back-and-forth lines. When you get to the edge of the quilting area, quilt the lines so they fit in the remaining space.

VARIATIONS

I love the texture that this design adds to a quilt. But if you want to change things up just a bit, try changing directions of the lines. Quilt one area with horizontal lines and quilt the next with vertical back-and-forth lines.

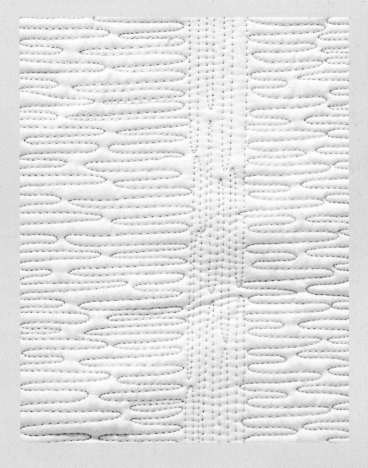

IMPROV QUILTING

Before you start quilting, take a moment to think about the different quilting designs you want to use. I usually decide on 3 or 4 designs. At least one of them needs to work as a filler design that can be quilted in a smaller scale compared with the others.

Some of my favorite designs to use include these:

Wavy lines, useful for breaking up the quilting area into smaller sections

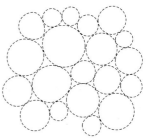

Pebbles, an ideal design to use as a filler

THE MODERN QUILT MOVEMENT IS WELL KNOWN FOR IMPROVISATIONAL PIECING. BUT I THINK WE CAN ALSO APPLY THAT TO MACHINE QUILTING. ONE OF MY FAVORITE THINGS TO DO IS "IMPROV QUILT," WHERE I PICK A FEW OF MY FAVORITE QUILTING DESIGNS AND THROW THEM TOGETHER. IT MAY LOOK COMPLETELY RANDOM, BUT THERE IS ACTUALLY A METHOD TO MY MADNESS. LET ME SHOW YOU!

Flowers, easy to execute with this design, which can grow to fit various sizes

note Don't worry about quilting the individual designs perfectly. It's more important that the quilting area is filled in completely.

TIP

This is a great way to practice a new design. Throw it in with some designs that you are more comfortable with, and get quilting!

Swirl chain (page 90), which we learned earlier in this chapter

When you begin quilting, quilt the larger designs first. For instance, quilt a flower or a larger swirl. Then, use your filler design to fill in the spaces between the larger designs.

A FEW IDEAS TO GET YOU STARTED

■ The more the merrier.

The best part of this technique is that you can go as crazy as you want! Instead of just picking three or four designs, try *many* of your favorite quilting designs. In the example below, I used feathers, flowers, pebbles, back-and-forth lines, swirls, and clamshells.

■ Get crazy small.

I always like to joke that if you want to impress people with your quilting, just quilt it crazy small. Although it's meant in jest, there is a bit of truth to it. In the example below, I used wavy lines to divide the quilting area into smaller sections, and then I quilted swirls, pebbles, and flowers between them.

■ Draw it.

If you aren't sure certain designs will play well together, take a moment and sketch it out. If it works when you draw it, then it will most likely work while quilting.

A WORD ABOUT THREAD

One concern I hear from other quilters is the fear that combining so many quilting designs could overwhelm the quilt top. Using a thread color that blends in with the quilt top will keep that from happening. In fact, I prefer to use blending thread in all of my quilting. No matter what quilt I am quilting, I don't want the quilting to overwhelm the quilt pattern.

section 3:
BORDERS

Quilted by Angela Walters

HERRINGBONE 106

BRACKETS 108

TRIANGLES 110

HALF BRACKETS 112

SERPENTINE LINE 114

WAVY VARIATION 116

WILD FEATHERS 118

ARCHES 120

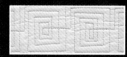

SQUARE CHAIN 122

DOT-TO-DOT 124
BORDERS

A border on a quilt top is like a frame to a picture...

a very important part of the quilt. The quilting designs you use in the borders of your quilt can add tremendous richness and detail. But what if you are like me and you're not so fond of quilting borders? Well then, these designs are definitely for you.

Personally, I try to avoid continuous designs for borders. Being able to break up a border design in chunks, or smaller pieces, allows you to quilt the border as you go, instead of all at once.

Tips for Quilting Borders

> DECIDE IF YOU WANT TO TREAT THE BORDER AS A SEPARATE PART OF THE QUILT by quilting a different design. You may prefer to extend the quilting designs used in other areas of the quilt into the border.

> BREAK UP THE BORDER INTO SMALLER SHAPES, such as squares or triangles, and use repeating designs from the corresponding chapter.

> DON'T BE AFRAID TO ADD TO (OR TAKE AWAY FROM) THE DESIGNS in this section. Make them as complex or as simple as you want!

> MAKE YOUR MARKING EASIER. While I usually try to avoid marking quilting designs, sometimes I need to quickly divide a border into sections. To do that, I use the Designs with Lines stencil (by Home Stitches) and a chalk pounce pad.

Ready to get quilting? Let's go!

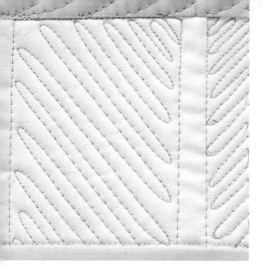

WHEN IT COMES TO QUILTING THE BORDERS OF A QUILT, I LOVE ANY DESIGN THAT BREAKS IT UP INTO SMALLER SECTIONS; THIS INCLUDES THE HERRINGBONE DESIGN. I LOVE EVERYTHING ABOUT IT. IT WORKS IN BORDERS OF ALL WIDTHS, AND CAN ADD AN INTRICATE, CUSTOM-QUILTED LOOK TO YOUR QUILT.

TO KEEP THE INDIVIDUAL SECTIONS THE SAME WIDTH, YOU COULD MARK THE DIVIDING LINES. HOWEVER, I FIND THAT EYEBALLING IT WILL GET YOU CLOSE ENOUGH!

HERRINGBONE

1. From the top corner of the border, travel along the edge approximately ½˝. Quilt a line down to the other side, travel along the bottom edge of the border, and quilt up to the top of the border.

2. Travel along the top edge of the border, returning to the top left corner of the rectangle. Fill in the rectangle with a diagonal back-and-forth line, ending at the opposite bottom corner.

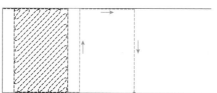

3. Travel along the bottom edge of the border about ½˝ and quilt the outside of another section by quilting up, to the right, and then down again.

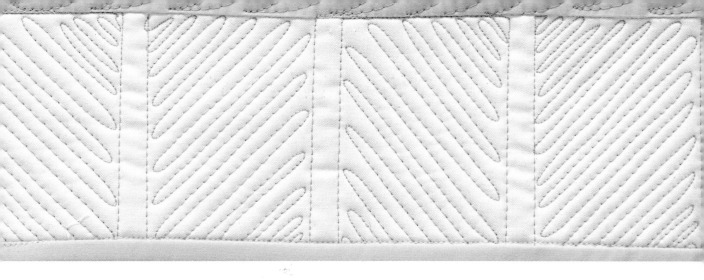

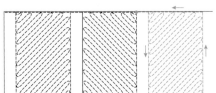

4. Travel along the bottom edge of the border, completing the section and filling in by quilting diagonal back-and-forth lines in the opposite direction of the first section.

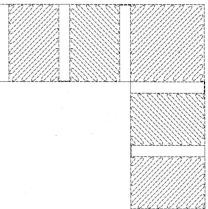

5. Repeat Steps 1–4 to fill the border with the sections to create the herringbone pattern.

This design is easy to quilt in the corners of a border as well, if you keep in mind the direction of the back-and-forth lines as you go.

VARIATIONS

If you don't particularly like the diagonal lines on this design, or you need a different look, here are a couple of options:

■ Make the separating lines closer or farther apart, depending on how dense you want the quilting to be.

■ Instead of quilting diagonal lines, try using a different filler design, such as a figure-eight or ribbon candy design.

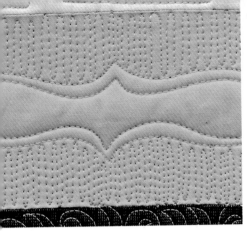

BRACKETS

1. Start on one edge of the border, slightly above the middle. Quilt a repeating bracket shape until you reach the edge of the border. Travel along the edge of the border approximately ½˝ and echo the brackets back to the beginning.

THIS DESIGN COMBINES TWO OF MY GO-TO DESIGNS: BRACKETS AND BACK-AND-FORTH LINES. IT'S A QUICK AND EASY DESIGN THAT CAN PACK QUITE A VISUAL PUNCH. THIS ADAPTABLE DESIGN FITS IN BORDERS OF ALL SIZES AND CAN ALSO WORK IN LARGER BLOCKS AND SASHING. TRY USING IT IN THE OUTER BORDERS OF A QUILT TO ADD A "FRAMED" EFFECT TO THE QUILT.

I don't mark the brackets; I just go for it. But you could consider marking a horizontal line along the border, so your line of brackets stays straight. You could also vary the spacing between the lines of brackets, depending on how dense you want the quilting.

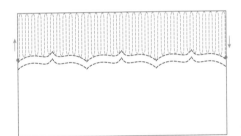

2. Quilt back-and-forth lines between the top of the brackets to the top of the border.

> **TIP**
> This design is quilted in several passes, but it is easily broken down into chunks. Follow along and manage each simple chunk to get a complex result.

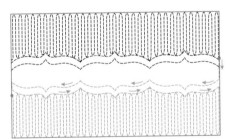

3. Once you reach the end of the border, travel along the edge until you are below the middle of the border. Repeat the technique in Steps 1 and 2 to quilt the bottom portion of the border.

I try to quilt the second row of brackets so they are a mirror image of the top row, but I don't stress out if it's not perfect!

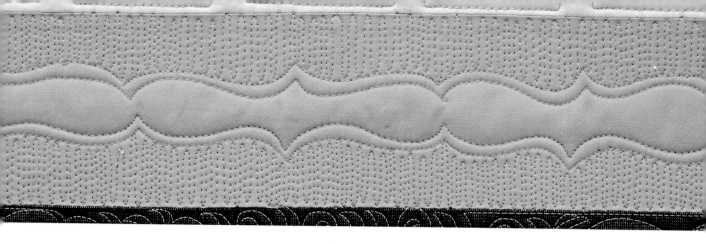

Corners

Quilting the brackets design so it wraps around a corner seamlessly is actually easier than it sounds. Before you start quilting, mark a line connecting the inner corner to the outer corner. When quilting the bracket lines, stop when you get to the marked line.

When quilting the back-and-forth lines, quilt them so they wrap around the corner.

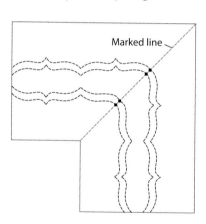

Marked line

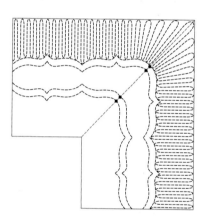

VARIATIONS

This design is quilted using several passes over the whole border. Sometimes, that isn't the most convenient way to quilt the border. If that is the case, quilt the bracket lines so they span the width of the border instead of the length.

Other Ways to Use the Brackets Border Design

Of course, there is no reason why you couldn't put your own twist on this fun design. Here are several ideas for how you could change this design to perfectly fit your situation:

- Consider using it as an allover design.

- Experiment with different widths between the back-and-forth lines.

- Instead of back-and-forth lines, try different designs, such as pebbles or dense swirls.

GIVE YOUR QUILT BORDERS A MORE GEO-
METRIC, JAGGED DESIGN BY QUILTING
TRIANGLES ALONG ONE EDGE OF THE
QUILT. THIS STRONG GRAPHIC DESIGN
WORKS BEST IN MEDIUM-SIZED BORDERS.
IF QUILTING LARGER BORDERS, CONSIDER
THROWING IN A CURVIER FREE-MOTION
QUILTING DESIGN AS A FILLER, TO
CREATE BALANCE AND CONTRAST!

BEFORE STARTING, DECIDE HOW
WIDE YOU WANT THE BASE OF THE
TRIANGLES. USING A MARKING PEN,
SUCH AS A WATER-SOLUBLE MARKER,
MAKE SMALL MARKS TO DIVIDE INTO
SECTIONS. OR, LOOK FOR A VISUAL
REFERENCE ON THE QUILT, SUCH
AS REPEATING QUILT BLOCKS.

TIP

When quilting diagonal lines
on my longarm, I almost
always use a ruler. I can't seem
to get diagonals nice and
smooth without it! If you are
quilting this on your sewing
machine, try positioning the
quilt so you are moving the
quilt back and forth.

TRIANGLES

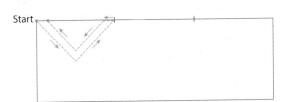

1. Starting
from a corner
of the border, quilt a diagonal line (roughly 45°) until
you are approximately halfway across the border. Quilt
diagonally in the opposite direction until you reach a
marked point on the top of the border.

Travel along the top of the border about ½˝ and echo
the inside of the triangle you just quilted.

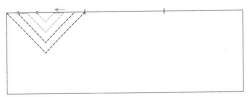

2. Continue
traveling and
echoing the inside of the triangle until it is filled.

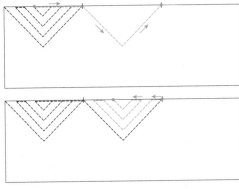

3. Travel along
the top of the
border until
you reach the
edge of the
first triangle
and repeat the technique in Steps 1 and 2 to continue
the border.

Corner Options

Since most borders wrap around the quilt, you may find that you need to adjust the design so that it fits. You can do this a couple of different ways:

- Instead of placing a triangle at the corner, quilt 3 sides of a square.

- Quilt the triangles so the end is on the corner.

VARIATIONS

If you need the triangles design to have a bit more oomph, try varying the spacing or angles of the triangle. Using a filler design as background for this border will really help the triangles stand out!

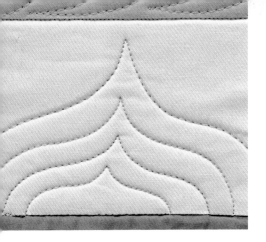

HALF BRACKETS

SOMETIMES, TO COME UP WITH A NEW DESIGN, ALL YOU NEED TO DO IS TAKE A FAVORITE DESIGN, DIVIDE IT IN HALF, AND REPEAT WITH A MIRROR IMAGE. SOUND CONFUSING? I PROMISE, IT ISN'T. SOON YOU WILL BE QUILTING HALF BRACKETS ON YOUR FAVORITE QUILTS. TRY QUILTING THIS DESIGN IN BORDERS OF ALL WIDTHS.

WHEN I AM QUILTING THE HALF BRACKET DESIGN ON MY QUILTS, I DON'T MARK THE SECTIONS. EVEN IF THEY AREN'T ALL THE SAME EXACT SIZE, THIS DESIGN STILL LOOKS GREAT!

1. Starting from one corner of the border, travel along the edge about ½˝. Quilt a curved line that comes to a point and then curves back to the border.

Try to have the half bracket shape come to a point before you reach the other side of the border. I usually like to leave about 1˝ or so.

2. Travel along the edge of the border about ¼˝ and echo inside the shape you just quilted. Keep traveling and echoing until you run out of space.

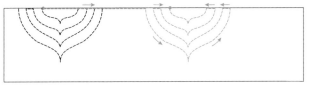

3. Travel along the edge of the border and leave a space about the same as the width of the half bracket. Repeat the technique in Steps 1 and 2 to create another set of half brackets.

Continue along the border, quilting the half brackets and spacing them evenly.

 **4.** Starting from the opposite edge of the border, repeat the process so that the half brackets fit between the ones on the top row.

VARIATIONS

Just like the other designs in this book, you can think up fun variations for this quilting design. Try quilting skinnier or wider half brackets, or quilt the echoed lines closer together.

If you want denser quilting, or really want to draw attention to this design, you could make another pass to fill in between the half brackets with pebbles.

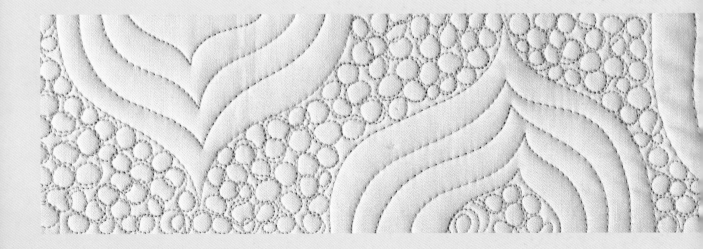

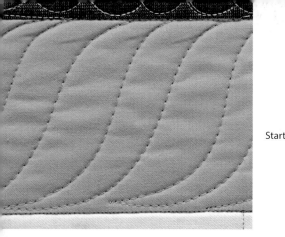

SERPENTINE LINE

A GREAT QUILTING DESIGN NEED NOT BE COMPLICATED. THIS CLEVER LITTLE DESIGN, SERPENTINE, IS ONE OF MY ALL-TIME FAVORITES! IT MAY LOOK BASIC, BUT IT REALLY PACKS A PUNCH. USE IT IN THINNER BORDERS AND SASHING FOR MAXIMUM EFFECT. GIVE IT A TRY AND SEE IF YOU LOVE IT AS MUCH AS I DO!

THE TRICKIEST PART OF QUILTING THIS DESIGN IS KEEPING THE SPACING CONSISTENT.

Start

1. From one corner of the border, quilt a serpentine-shaped line at an angle, ending on the opposite side of the border.

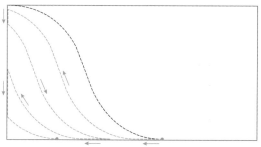

2. Before you continue quilting along the border, fill in the space between the edge of the border and the first line by echoing the line. Travel along the edge, and continue echoing the serpentine shape.

TIP
Quilt each line so it runs into the edge of the border. This will help you keep the spacing consistent between lines.

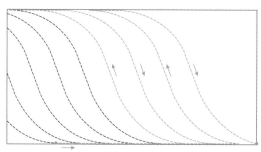

3. Once the space is filled, travel along the edge of the border until you are on the other side of the first line you quilted. Work your way across the border, repeating the serpentine shape.

Corners

This design is pretty straightforward until it's time to work your way around a corner. But once you get the hang of it, it will be smooth sailing.

When you get into the corner of your border, you will need to quilt the serpentine lines so they are more spread out at the top and closer at the inner corner.

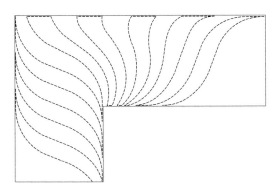

VARIATIONS

Ready to add your own flair to this design? Here are a few ideas for variations.

- Before quilting the serpentine lines, quilt straight lines that echo the sides of the borders. This will make the serpentine lines really stand out!

- Change the angle. I tend to quilt the design at 45° (at least I try to), but you can make it more horizontal or vertical, depending on your preferences.

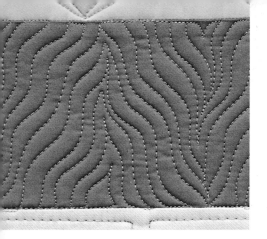

WAVY VARIATION

WAVY LINES ARE EASY AND FAST TO QUILT, BUT SOMETIMES A QUILT NEEDS A LITTLE MORE THAN JUST REGULAR WAVY LINES. THIS DESIGN TAKES THE BASIC WAVY LINE AND ALTERNATES THE DIRECTION TO CREATE AN INTERESTING VISUAL EFFECT. THIS DESIGN IS ALSO QUILTED IN SECTIONS, WHICH MEANS YOU CAN QUILT THE BORDER AS YOU MAKE YOUR WAY DOWN THE QUILT.

WHEN QUILTING THIS DESIGN, YOU DEFINITELY DON'T WANT TO MARK THE LINES. THE FLUID, ORGANIC LOOK OF THIS DESIGN IS WHAT MAKES IT SO GREAT!

note This design is in the border section of the book because it goes from edge to edge. But you could use it in larger quilt blocks as well.

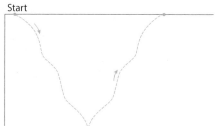

1. From one corner of the border, quilt a gently waving line diagonally until you reach the other side of the border. Quilt back up to the top of the border at an angle.

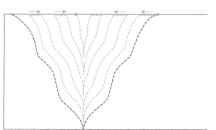

2. Travel along the top of the border approximately ½˝; then echo the inside of the V. Continue traveling and echoing until the space is completely filled.

note When echoing the inside of the V shape, quilt the lines so they are almost touching at the points but are about ¼˝ to ½˝ apart at the edge of the border. This is what gives the design a groovy look!

3. When finished with the first V, travel along the edge of the border until you are at the edge of the V. From that point, quilt a diagonal wavy line until it touches the opposite edge of the border.

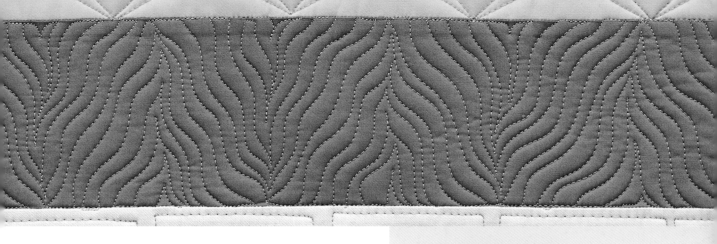

VARIATIONS

This design is so fast and fun that you might not need any variations. But just in case, here are a few ideas of how you can give this design a little makeover.

- Try quilting the V shapes wider and more spread out.

- Instead of keeping the V shapes the same size, vary the widths. Try alternating skinnier and wider V's for an even more organic look.

- Try this design in a large square so that each side of the square is the wide part of a V.

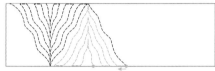

4. Repeat Steps 1 and 2 to fill in the V.

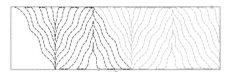

5. Work your way across the border, quilting alternating V shapes and filling them in with the wavy lines.

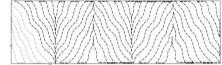

When starting or finishing a border, you will have a half V. Fill those spaces by echoing one side of the V.

This design looks amazing in the corners of a border as well.

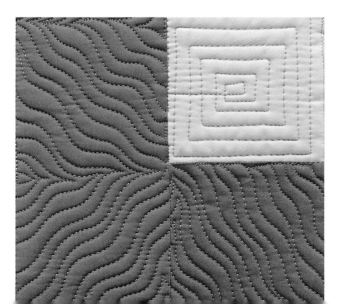

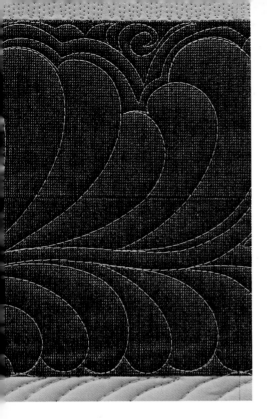

WILD FEATHERS

Start

1. From a random spot on one edge of the border, quilt a gently waving line that extends to the opposite edge.

note Don't feel as though you need to quilt the line the same as I did in the illustration. The more random and curvy you make the line, the wilder your feathers will be.

2. Quilt the first "petal" of your feather by quilting a line that goes out and curves down, touching the edge of the border.

3. Travel along the curve of the petal until you are almost past the widest part, then quilt the next petal by curving up and back to the spine.

TIP

For perfect petals, quilt them so they tuck down into the spine of the feather.

4. Travel up the spine and then quilt your next petal. Repeat this technique to quilt petals up the spine until you reach the top.

I LOVE FEATHERS AND USE THEM ON A LOT OF MY QUILTS. BUT I REALLY DON'T CARE FOR QUILTING CONTINUOUS FEATHERS IN THE BORDER OF A QUILT. SO INSTEAD, I BREAK THEM UP AND LET THEM GO WILD ON THE BORDERS. NOT ONLY DOES THIS ALLOW ME TO EASILY QUILT THE BORDER AS I GO, BUT IT GIVES THE FEATHER A WILD, MORE RANDOM LOOK!

note There are many different ways to quilt feathers, but this is my favorite!

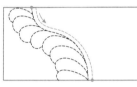

5. Echo down the other side of the spine.

note You don't have to quilt all the petals the same size. Try quilting petals of varying sizes for an even wilder look.

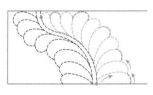

6. Quilt petals along that side of the feather.

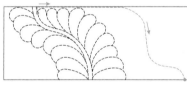

7. Travel along the edge of the border and quilt another wavy line for the next feather. Make sure to leave yourself enough space to add the petals.

VARIATIONS

Echo the feathers and use a filler quilting design, such as swirls, to fill in between your wild feathers.

TIP

Using a dense swirl quilting design will really help show off your feathers!

ARCHES

THIS DESIGN INVOLVES A TEENY BIT OF MARKING, BUT DON'T LET THAT DISSUADE YOU FROM TRYING IT. THE ARCHES DESIGN IS FAST TO QUILT AND LOOKS GREAT IN SMALLER-TO MEDIUM-WIDTH BORDERS.

note I use a Designs with Lines stencil to quickly mark the sections of a border.

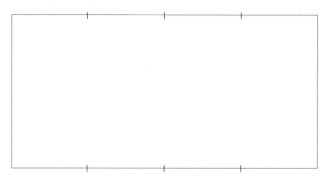

1. Before you start quilting, you will need to do a little marking. Depending on how wide you want the arches, divide the border into equal sections. For most borders, I use 2˝ sections. But you don't need to mark the whole line across the border, just a tick mark at the top and bottom edge of the border.

TIP

Instead of marking the spacing, try to find visual reference points on the quilt, such as seams or quilt blocks.

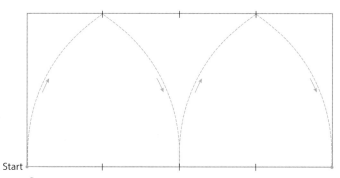

Start

2. Starting from one corner of the border, quilt a curved line that comes to a point at the next tick mark at the top of the border and back down to the bottom of the border. Work across the border, alternating between the top and bottom.

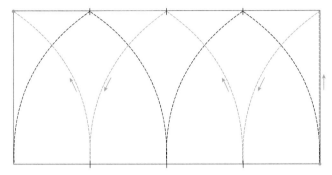

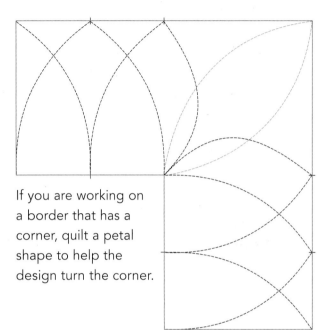

3. Once you are at the edge of the border, travel along the edge to the top and work your way back across the border, alternating between the marked points. The arches should overlap.

If you are working on a border that has a corner, quilt a petal shape to help the design turn the corner.

VARIATIONS

To give these arches a different look, quilt the arches in opposite directions. It is not always easy to imagine what tweaking a design will do to it, so you need to try it out!

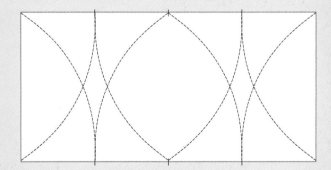

SQUARE CHAIN

TIP

What about rulers? For quilting designs with shorter straight lines, such as the square chain, try quilting without a ruler. This will save you valuable time.

THIS DESIGN IS THE HARDEST-WORKING DESIGN IN MY TOOLBOX. I USE IT ALL THE TIME—IT FITS ALL WIDTHS OF BORDERS AND SASHING, FROM SKINNY TO REALLY WIDE, NOT TO MENTION THE FACT THAT NO MARKING IS REQUIRED! NOT ONLY WILL I SHOW YOU HOW TO QUILT THE REGULAR SQUARE CHAIN, BUT I WILL SHOW YOU A VARIATION THAT WILL HOPEFULLY BECOME YOUR FAVORITE AS WELL!

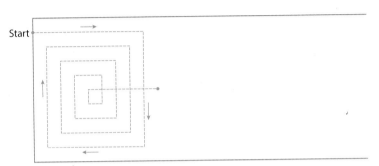

Start

1. Starting from one side of the border, quilt a square that echoes in on itself until you get to the center. Quilt across the square until you are about ½″ outside of the square.

note I usually keep the echo lines about ¼″ apart, but you can make them as close or as spread out as you want!

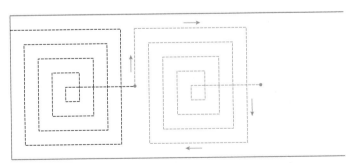

2. Quilt a vertical line going up to align with the first square. Continue quilting the border by quilting repeating squares.

VARIATIONS

If you want to quilt more than just straight lines, try this variation, which combines the square chain design with swirls. This is using the best of both worlds!

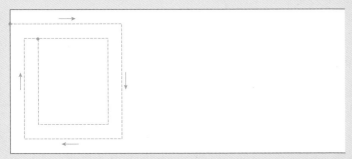

1. As you did for the square chain, start by quilting the outside of a square. Echo once around the inside of the square, stopping so the line touches the side of the square.

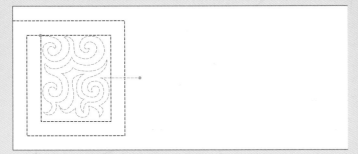

2. Quilt a swirl meander that fills the square, ending in the middle of the opposite side of the square. Quilt a straight line across the square.

3. Repeat the technique in Steps 1 and 2 and quilt squares across the border.

DOT-TO-DOT BORDERS

I COULDN'T WRITE A SECTION OF BORDER DESIGNS WITHOUT HAVING ONE THAT USES STRAIGHT LINES! THIS DESIGN USES POINTS ON THE BORDER TO CREATE A COMPLEX-LOOKING DESIGN. IT LOOKS A LOT HARDER THAN IT IS, TRUST ME. ALL YOU HAVE TO DO IS MARK AND CONNECT THE DOTS!

JUST AS YOU DID WITH THE ARCHES QUILTING DESIGN (PAGE 120), YOU WILL NEED TO DO A BIT OF MARKING. DIVIDE THE BORDER INTO EQUAL SECTIONS USING TICK MARKS. FOR THIS DESIGN, I USUALLY DIVIDE IT INTO 2″ OR 3″ SECTIONS.

1. Starting from one corner of the border, quilt a diagonal line to the next mark on the bottom edge, and the back up to the next mark. Repeat until you get to the edge of the border.

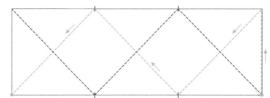

2. Travel along the edge of the border to the top corner, and quilt back to the other side of the border. You will have what looks like a row of X's.

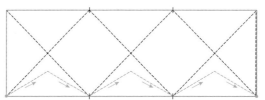

3. Now we are going to fill in the bottom of the X's. Quilt a line diagonally until you are about ½″ from the center of the X, then quilt diagonally to the next mark. Repeat until you have worked your way across the border.

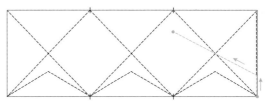

4. Travel along the edge of the border about ½″ and quilt a diagonal line that crosses through the center of the first X, stopping ½″ from the mark at the top of the border.

5. Work your way across the border, quilting diagonal lines that cross at the X's.

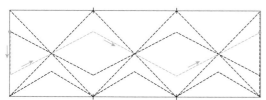

6. Travel down the side of the border until you are about ½″ from the bottom corner of the border; repeat Step 5. Continue until you reach the opposite side of the border.

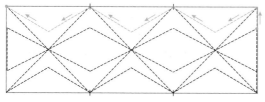

7. Almost done! Travel along the edge of the border until you are at the top corner. Repeat the technique in Step 3, filling in the top of the X's.

VARIATIONS

If you are working on a larger border, or are an overachiever, you could add a free-motion quilting design between the shapes you just quilted.

In this example, I used a figure-eight quilting design, but you could try other dense fillers such as pebbles or swirls.

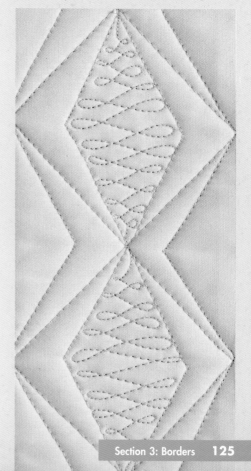

CONCLUSION

At this point, your head is probably swirling with possibilities! While this is only a sampling of machine-quilting designs available, my hope is that these designs and the variations (or better yet, your own variations) will help you grow your collection of favorite machine-quilting designs.

Happy quilting!

ABOUT THE AUTHOR

Angela Walters is a machine quilter and author who loves to teach others to use quilting to bring out the best in their quilts. Her work has been published in numerous magazines and books. She shares tips and finished quilts on her blog, quiltingismytherapy.com, and believes that "quilting is the funnest part!"

ALSO BY ANGELA WALTERS

stashBOOKS

fabric arts for a handmade lifestyle

If you're craving beautiful authenticity in a time of mass-production...Stash Books is for you. Stash Books is a line of how-to books celebrating fabric arts for a handmade lifestyle. Backed by C&T Publishing's solid reputation for quality, Stash Books will inspire you with contemporary designs, clear and simple instructions, and engaging photography.

www.stashbooks.com